A Date with the Hangman

A Date with the Hangman

Hangman

A History of Capital Punishment in Britain

Gary Dobbs

PEN & SWORD
HISTORY

AN IMPRINT OF PEN & SWORD BOOKS LTD.
YORKSHIRE - PHILADELPHIA

First published in Great Britain in 2019 by
Pen & Sword History
An imprint of
Pen & Sword Books Ltd
Yorkshire - Philadelphia

Copyright © Gary Dobbs, 2019

Hardback ISBN 978 1 52674 743 3
Paperback ISBN 978 1 52676 740 0

Printed and bound in England
By TJ International Ltd.

Pen & Sword Books Ltd incorporates the Imprints of Pen & Sword Books
Archaeology, Atlas, Aviation, Battleground, Discovery, Family History, History,
Maritime, Military, Naval, Politics, Railways, Select, Transport, True Crime,
Fiction, Frontline Books, Leo Cooper, Praetorian Press, Seaforth Publishing,
Wharncliffe and White Owl.

For a complete list of Pen & Sword titles please contact

PEN & SWORD BOOKS LIMITED
47 Church Street, Barnsley, South Yorkshire, S70 2AS, England
E-mail: enquiries@pen-and-sword.co.uk
Website: www.pen-and-sword.co.uk

or

PEN AND SWORD BOOKS
1950 Lawrence Rd, Havertown, PA 19083, USA
E-mail: uspen-and-sword@casematepublishers.com
Website: www.penandswordbooks.com

'Executions are so much a part of British history that it is almost impossible for many excellent people to think of a future without them.'

Samuel John Hoare, *In the Shadow of the Gallows* (1951)

Contents

Introduction

It is a sobering thought that until the closing years of the twentieth century, Britain's courts were technically able to impose the death penalty for a number of offences; both civil and military. And although the last judicial hangings took place in 1964, the death penalty, in theory at least, remained for a number of offences. It would not be completely abolished until 1998, and even then it wasn't until 2004, when the European Convention on Human Rights became binding on the United Kingdom, that the slim possibility that capital punishment could be restored was removed.

Although the main focus of this book is a study of British judicial hangings during the twentieth century, in which all 865 executions carried out between the years 1900 and 1964 are detailed, it is important to consider this overall history of the death penalty as it relates to the judiciary. And so, to truly understand capital punishment and its eventual abolishment, one must go beyond judicial sentencing and look at the whole picture; the origins of why hanging became the preferred method of punishment for the most heinous of crimes.

It is thought that hanging as a capital punishment was first brought to Britain in the latter half of the fifth century by the Anglo Saxons, but throughout history people have been burned at the stake, had the skin flayed from their bodies, been beheaded, garrotted, hung, drawn and quartered, stoned, disembowelled, buried alive, all under the guidance of a vengeful law, or at least what passed for law at any given period.

However, with the arrival of the Germanic Anglo-Saxon tribes, hanging at the gallows became the principle form of judicial execution. The gallows were an important element of Germanic culture. Indeed, the legendary brothers Hengist and Horsa, whom history records as leading the invasion of Britain in the fifth century, used a very rough version of a gallows for hanging. It is from here that the accepted method of hanging developed.

In 1066 when William the Conqueror became the first Norman King of England, he decreed that hanging should be replaced by castration and blinding for all but the crimes of poaching royal deer. Hanging would later be reintroduced by Henry I as a means of execution for a larger number of x A Date with the Hangman

offences, although during this period in history other methods of execution such as beheading, burning at the stake and being boiled alive were also used. In fact it wasn't until the eighteenth century that hanging had become the principle punishment for capital crimes in the United Kingdom.

The eighteenth century would also see the start of the movement to abolish capital punishment, and in 1770 the politician William Meredith suggested that more proportionate punishments for crimes be introduced. He was joined in the early nineteenth century by the legal reformer and Solicitor General Samuel Romilly, and the Scottish jurist, politician and historian James Mackintosh, both of whom introduced bills into Parliament in attempts to de-capitalise minor crimes. At this time there were more than 200 crimes defined in law as capital offences; among these were impersonating a Chelsea pensioner, being found in a forest while disguised, and damaging Westminster Bridge. During this period the law did not distinguish between adults and children, and it was not uncommon for children as young as 7 to be sent to the gallows. It would not be until 1861, with the Criminal Law Consolidation Act, that the number of capital crimes was reduced to just four, these being murder, arson in a royal dockyard, treason and piracy with violence.

A hundred years later, Britain would finally take steps to end capital punishment with the last judicial executions taking place in August 1964, when both Peter Anthony Allen and Gwynne Owen Evans were executed for the joint murder of John Alan West. These men were executed at separate prisons at precisely 8am on 13 August. There was little outcry, few headlines and yet these two men would go down in history as the last men to face the hangmen in the United Kingdom.

Chapter One

Beheading: Punishment and the Nobility

Although the Celts, regarded by many historians as being the first inhabitants of the British Isles, had a long tradition of beheading, the first recorded judicial execution did not take place until the third century AD. This was during the Roman occupation; indeed, the Romans regarded beheading as the only humane form of execution. It was seen as being the least painful way of putting someone to death, and in most cases was reserved for the nobility and seldom used on common criminals. Mark Anthony's grandfather and son were executed in this way, as was the famous statesman Cicero.

The *Anglo-Saxon Chronicles* tell us that the first judicial beheading to be properly recorded took place in AD 283, although experts debate the actual date with opinion placing the event sometime between AD 209 and 313. During this period Christianity was being suppressed by the Roman rulers and a persecuted Christian priest named Amphibalus took refuge with a young man named Alban. This was in the city of Verulamium, situated to the south-west of modern-day St. Albans, and in order for the priest to evade capture, Alban exchanged clothes with the man. This resulted in Alban being seized and executed in place of the priest. He was beheaded with a sword on the site that would later house St. Alban's Abbey. There are many differing accounts of the execution, most written hundreds of years after the fact. One report, written by the Benedictine monk, Bede, states that Alban's head rolled down a small hill, and where it stopped a well suddenly sprung up from the ground. References to this spontaneous well are recorded in local place names such as Halywell, which in Middle English would mean Holy Well. The hill leading to where the abbey now stands is called Holywell Hill, but it has been called Halliwell Street and other variations since at least the thirteenth century.

Beheading would continue for the next eight centuries, both the Anglo Saxons and Vikings favouring this form of punishment, but it was not until William I invaded Britain in 1066 that beheading became a truly respectable form of capital punishment. The first recorded victim was Waltheof, Earl of

Northumberland, who had been a leading voice in the Revolt of the Earls against William's rule. Convicted of treason he was executed at St. Giles Hill near Winchester on 30 May 1076. This event started the British tradition of cutting the heads off noblemen and women who opposed the monarchy.

The most common method of beheading became the axe and block, which was preferable to using a sword, as in earlier executions, because it required only brute strength, rather than any special skill on the part of the executioner. There were two types of blocks used for beheading: the low and the high block. The high block was considered the best since it allowed the condemned to kneel gracefully and lay his or her head on the block. The low block was really only used when resistance was expected, since it was easier this way to hold the condemned in place while the axeman swung his axe. It was harder though for the executioner to swing his axe at the correct angle, and executions using the low block would often involve more than one cut with the axe to separate head from body.

It is interesting and also quite remarkable, quintessentially British even, that it was assumed that those about to lose their heads would behave with the correct decorum, play their part sportingly and not struggle against the inevitable. Most of those sentenced to death in this way belonged to the upper classes, and they were expected to face death with more detachment than people of lower social standing, and for the most part this was how it worked out. However, there were exceptions and these could be quite tragic.

The execution of Margaret Pole, Countess of Salisbury, in May 1541 is one example. She was a lady-in-waiting to Henry VIII's first wife Catherine of Aragon, and her family had been a part of the aristocracy from early times. One of her five children was Reginald Pole, who would become a cardinal and then Archbishop of Canterbury during the reign of Mary I. In 1534 following the Pope's statement that Henry's marriage to Anne Boleyn was invalid, Henry VIII broke away from Rome, becoming the head of the Church of England. There was much opposition to this move which gave the King supreme power over the English church, as well as the considerable wealth and land owned by the church. Reginald Pole spoke out against the King, stating that his divorce from Catherine of Aragon had no legal standing, and when he later published *Pro ecclesiasticae unitatis defensione*, which denounced Henry's policies, the King was furious. In November of 1538 various members of the Pole family were seized and charged with treason. Margaret Pole would spend two years in the Tower of London before she was executed. There are differing accounts of the execution but it is known that it took eleven blows of the axe to remove her head. She was 67 years of age and it must have been a pitiful sight as the old woman, reportedly confused, was led to the block. She refused to place her head in the required position and instead struggled fiercely with her captors. The first swing of the axe merely gashed her shoulder, and she screamed in pain, continuing to struggle until ten more blows had been struck and she was finally dead.

Another famous botched execution took place in 1685 when James Scott, Duke of Monmouth, who had led a rebellion against James II, was beheaded at the Tower. Upon being led to the block, Scott examined the blade and feared it was not sharp enough to do the job cleanly. He gave the executioner, Jack Ketch, a man whose name is synonymous with hangmen and executioners, a purse containing seven guineas and asked him to do the job with one blow, and the executioner assured him that all was well and that he would feel little pain. The Duke though did feel pain. The first blow glanced off the back of his head, and after another two blows his head was still attached to his body. At this point Jack Ketch threw down his axe, saying that he could not finish the job, but he was ordered back to the grisly task and it took a further two blows before the job was done. Some accounts claim that the job was finished with a knife and that there were eight blows of the axe, but the official Tower of London fact sheet states that it took five blows.

There were many cases of the condemned going calmly to meet their fate and even offering witty remarks on the grisly end that awaited them. Sir Walter Raleigh for instance asked to see the axe before his execution and ran his finger over its fine edge, remarking, 'It is sharp medicine but a sure remedy for all ills.'

Thomas Moore asked for help to be led to the scaffold but said that he would find his own way down afterwards. And when it was time for him to lay his head upon the block he moved his beard out of the way, stating that his beard had committed no act of treason and should not suffer the same fate as the rest of him.

There were many places designated for executions in Britain, though the most widely used was the area outside the Tower of London. Private executions were carried out at Tower Green, situated within the walls of the Tower, while public events were staged at Tower Hill. Other areas of London were Lincoln's Inn Fields, Smithfield and Tyburn. Kensington Common also became a popular venue for public beheadings. Further afield, York saw several beheadings throughout history, and there were venues in Wales and Scotland.

Perhaps the most famous beheading of them all was that of Charles I, which took place in the very heart of Westminster: outside the banqueting house in Whitehall. So important to the history of capital punishment was this event that we shall now examine it in detail.

When the English Civil War came to an end in 1647, Charles I was held by the victorious Parliamentary forces. While in captivity the King engaged in secret negotiations with Scotland, encouraging his Scottish supporters to invade England. So began the second civil war and the King's holders realised that they would never be able to release the monarch. There had been hopes that he could have been returned to power once his differences with Parliament had been resolved, but this now became impossible and Parliament took the unprecedented move of putting the King on trial for treason. While kings of England had been deposed and put to death before, these had been murders rather than judicial executions. The trial of Charles I was quite different. He was charged with treason against his own people because he had put his own selfish needs before those of the greater good. The legality of these charges has been debated through the centuries and continue to be so to the present day, but the result was that on 27 January 1649, Charles I, now referred to simply as Charles Stuart, was found guilty of treason and sentenced to death by beheading.

He was taken to St James's Palace while arrangements for his execution were made. The authorities had considerable trouble finding someone to swing the axe. Richard Brandon, then the London hangman, was offered the task for considerable reward but he refused fearing retribution from the King's supporters, though he did claim on his deathbed that he had carried out the execution. Some reports claim that two relatively inexperienced men were recruited for the job. Whatever the truth, the executioner and his assistant both wore masks, ensuring their anonymity. This would prove prudent in light of the savage retribution against all those connected following the restoration of the monarchy in 1660.

The execution took place on the morning of 30 January 1649. The King was led from the palace to Whitehall where a scaffold had been erected. A low block was used as it was expected the monarch would fight until the last, so he was forced to lie face down on the straw-covered floor and then was securely bound to the scaffold. As it turned out the King would maintain his dignity, showing tremendous courage right up to the moment his head left his body. He asked the executioner if his hair was set well and then told him he would like to say a prayer before the axe was swung: 'When I put my hands this way,' the King was reported as saying in contemporary accounts, 'that will be the signal to strike.'

Charles then laid his head on the block and began to pray. Upon hearing the executioner shifting his weight, the King warned, 'Stay for the sign'.

'I will if it please your majesty,' the executioner replied.

A few seconds later the King gave the sign and the axe swung down at once, cleanly severing the head with one blow. The head dropped into a zinc-lined basket that had been placed to receive it.

As we have noted, executions by beheading were largely reserved for nobility. When commoners were granted this type of death it was largely seen as a favour for services they may have once performed for the authorities. One such case was that of Mark Smeaton, who had been a musician at the court of Henry VIII and was convicted of treason because of his love affair with Ann Boleyn. When he was found guilty and sentenced to death it was expected he would be hung, drawn and quartered – the usual method of executing commoners charged with treason. However, Smeaton had cooperated fully during his interrogation, giving much evidence for Thomas Cromwell and King Henry VIII to use against Anne, and he was granted the relatively humane death of beheading. He was executed at Tyburn on 17 May 1536.

For the nobility, execution was made as dignified as was possible under the circumstances. Guards and gaolers would address them by their correct titles. The proceedings were polite and formal and there would invariably be an opportunity for the condemned to make a final speech to those who had gathered to view the execution. In many cases the condemned would praise the mercy of the monarch and acknowledge the justice of their sentence. There may have been good reason for this as many of those executed had families. If it was thought that those left behind felt aggrieved by the court's verdict and thus represented a threat to the Crown, then they too would be dealt with harshly. By agreeing that it was right for them to die for their crimes, the condemned might avert future retribution.

Thomas Cromwell for instance, who was beheaded in 1540, declared before his execution: 'The devil is ready to seduce us and I have been seduced, but bear witness that I die in the Catholic faith of the Holy Church and I heartily desire you to pray for the King's grace. That he may long live in health and prosperity, and that after him his son Edward may long reign over you.'

It was in 1747 that the last public judicial beheading took place in Britain. The condemned man was Simon Frazer, the 11th Lord Lovat, who was sentenced to death by beheading over his part in the Jacobite uprisings of 1746. He had originally been sentenced to the traitor's punishment of being hanged, drawn and quartered, but this was later commuted by the King to beheading. On the morning of 9 April he awoke in his cell at 5am and spent an hour in prayer. He then ate a good breakfast of minced veal and invited several friends to take coffee with him. He was 80 years of age and grossly overweight, unable to walk more than a few feet unaided, but his execution was carried out with great decorum and civility. He was allowed to have several friends accompany him to the scaffold, where he gave the executioner a purse containing ten guineas. He said he would pray on the block for several moments and when he was ready, he would drop a handkerchief; that would be the signal. The execution went smoothly, a single blow of the axe taking the head clean off.

Severed heads were usually put on display to deter others from conspiring against the Crown. At this time London Bridge had many shops, drinking establishments and houses along its length, and on the Southwark end of the bridge heads were displayed for all those who walked across to see.

Viewing the heads on the bridge was especially popular with the poor, as they could see the faces of noble-born people they could never hope to come across in the usual run of their lives. The newly installed head of a prominent person would bring vast crowds on its first day.

From the early fourteenth century the heads of prominent traitors were also displayed from a gateway in Fleet Street. This gateway was demolished in the seventeenth century when Sir Christopher Wren was commissioned to design a new one. This new gateway at Temple Bar was also used to display the heads and other body parts of traitors who had been put to death.

The last heads to be put on display at Temple Bar belonged to nine men who had taken arms against the Crown during the 1745 rebellion. They had been hung, drawn and quartered at Kensington Common. Two of them, Colonel Townley and a man named Fletcher, had their heads treated with tar to preserve them. The heads were then skewered on a long iron bar and placed on display at Temple Bar. They remained there for a quarter of a century only to finally fall down during a thunderstorm in 1772. One head rolled along the street until it bumped into the legs of a woman who promptly fainted. The Temple Bar gateway still stands today, though it has been removed several times and currently resides next to St Paul's Cathedral.

Hanging, drawing and quartering was abolished by the 1870 Forfeiture Act, which made ordinary hanging the mandatory sentence for high treason. The act removed the rights of the monarchy to substitute hanging with decapitation, but judicial beheading remained, in theory, a possible sentence right up until the late twentieth century. It wasn't until the Statute Law (Repeals) Act of 1973 that the right of a reigning monarch to insist on beheading was removed entirely from law.

Chapter Two

Crime and Punishment: A Myriad of Ways to Die

Hanging would not become Britain's principle method of judicial execution until the nineteenth century, and in this chapter we will examine some of the horrendous ways in which a vengeful law has historically punished wrongdoers sentenced to death.

Breaking on the Wheel

This method of execution, although common on the continent, was seldom used in Britain. The condemned would be tied spreadeagled to a cartwheel, or a wooden cross, and the executioner would use a hammer to smash the limbs in two places. The upper and lower arms would be broken, and the same would be done with the legs. Then the person would be left in agony for however long the courts specified before the merciful release of death. Sometimes the wheel would be turned. For simple murder the condemned would usually be killed immediately after the limbs were broken.

There are two recorded cases of this particularly barbaric punishment being carried out in Scotland. In Edinburgh in 1604, Robert Weir was broken on the wheel for his part in the murder of John Kinkaid a few years earlier. Two others had been accomplices in the murder, Kincaid's wife Jean had been beheaded immediately following the murder, and an unnamed female servant had been burned alive. Weir had escaped justice by fleeing only to be captured in 1603. He was broken on the wheel in June of 1604 and allowed to suffer for several hours before death was brought about by strangulation.

The only other recorded case of breaking on the wheel was also in Scotland. In 1591 John Dickson, convicted of parricide, was broken on the wheel and allowed to suffer for one full night before being put to death. Afterwards his body was hung on a gibbet.

Boiled Alive

Being boiled in a cauldron was prescribed in Tudor law for killing by poisoning, considered a particularly terrible crime, and in 1531 a man named Richard Roose was the cook to the Bishop of Rochester. He attempted to poison the bishop but ended up killing several members of the household instead. Roose was sentenced to be boiled alive in a cauldron and this took place in public at Smithfield. One contemporary account stated, 'He roared mighty loud, and women who were big with child did feel sick at the sight of what they saw and were carried away half dead; and other men and women did not seem frightened by the boiling alive but would prefer to see the headsman at his work.' Roose, trussed up and unable to move, had been placed into the cauldron while the water was still cold and it took a considerable time for him to die. In 1542, a maid who had poisoned members of the household where she lived was also boiled alive at Smithfield.

When King Edward VI took the throne in 1547, boiling alive as a method of execution was removed from law.

Pressing to Death

The condemned man or woman was stretched out on their back, with ropes securing the arms and legs to posts or rings. A wooden board was then placed on the chest and weights were placed upon the board until death occurred. If a person was guilty of a crime that was considered particularly evil then enough weight was placed on the board to cause great agony but not death, until such time that it was felt they had suffered enough when more weights were added to bring about the merciful release of death. Originally this procedure, officially sanctioned in 1275, was intended to coerce a confession or plea from accused persons. The legal term for this was 'mute of malice', which described the problem of accused persons refusing to plead at their trial. They would be taken away to a small cell and crushed until they agreed to offer a plea. Once they had done so, their trial would continue as normal.

There are many cases of pressing in British history. One of the most famous occurred in 1586 when Margaret Clitheroe was pressed to death at York. She was an ardent Catholic, who during the reign of Elizabeth I was arrested for harbouring Catholic priests at her home, which was technically treason. She was brought before the York Assizes, but she refused to plead. She knew full well the consequences of refusing to plead, but feared that if she was brought to trail her children would be called as witnesses. If they then refused to give evidence against their mother, as they were likely to do, then they too could find themselves tortured. Far better, Margaret decided, to allow herself to be pressed to death so that there would be no trial. On 25 March, Good Friday that year, Margaret, who was pregnant with her fourth child, was stretched out with a sharp stone said to be the size of a man's fist under her back. This was considered a merciful variation on the usual procedure since the stone was designed to break her back and bring about death quicker than usual. Eight hundred pounds of stone was placed on the board before, after fifteen minutes, she died. There was an outcry following the execution and Elizabeth I was forced to write to the citizens of York stating that Clitheroe should not have been executed. Seen as a martyr for her faith, Margaret Clitheroe was later canonised and is now a saint of the Catholic Church. Her shrine stands in The Shambles, York, and there is also a plaque marking the place of her execution at the Micklegate end of York's Ouse Bridge.

Burning at the Stake

For centuries being burned at the stake was the prescribed punishment for a number of offences. There is a common misconception that women convicted of witchcraft were usually punished in this way. The facts are that in England and Wales those convicted of witchcraft were for the most part hanged, and although Scotland did impose the penalty of burning for witchcraft, it was hardly commonplace. In his book *Witchfinders* (2005), Malcolm Gaskill reveals that only three women were burned for witchcraft in England between 1440 and 1560 but more than 200 were hanged for the offence.

Executions by being burnt alive were recorded by Julius Caesar. In *The Gallic Wars* he wrote that the Celts built huge wickerwork figures and then filled them with convicted criminals and set fire to them. The Bible prescribes death by burning for a number of crimes, notably sexual immorality. The Bible also states that sinners will burn for all eternity, and this likely led to the Catholic Church declaring in 1184 that death by burning should be adopted as the official penalty for heresy. This was seen as a particularly terrible punishment since most people believed in a physical resurrection after death; being reduced to little more than ashes would surely rule out the possibility of rising from the grave. This reasoning seemed logical to people at the time; those who lost limbs would preserve them to the best of their ability so that they would eventually be buried with them, in the belief that come Judgement Day their limbs would once again become a part of their body.

The reign of Henry V saw the passing of the 1414 Heresy Act, which amended the previous 1401 act made during the reign of King Henry IV by recategorizing the offence of heresy as a civil as well as an ecclesiastical offence. This meant that those found guilty would be hanged for treason against the King and then burned for heresy against God.

In 1441 Margery Jourdemayne was accused of trying to kill King Henry VI by means of witchcraft. But she was found guilty of treason and heresy rather than witchcraft, and was burned alive on 27 October that year. This event would be immortalized by Shakespeare in part two of his Henry VI trilogy.

Regular judicial burnings continued in this country and would continue to do so after King Henry VIII repealed the 1401 Act, ensuring that those charged with heresy would now be indicted through the normal courts. This was another move by the King to remove powers from the Church which would eventually lead to the dissolution of the monasteries and the establishment of the Anglican Church. Between 1509 and 1547 more than eighty people were burnt for heresy in England.

In London burnings at the stake were usually carried out at Smithfield, where the meat market now stands. For the person facing such a fate the best that could be hoped for was that they would quickly lose consciousness through inhaling carbon monoxide, but many accounts exist of people dying in hideous pain while the flames consumed their flesh.

Drawing and Quartering

Drawing and quartering was only used on those guilty of what was considered the most despicable crime of all: treason. Treason was for many centuries viewed as being far worse than murder since it challenged the God-given order. The punishment took place in several steps and was always carried out in public in front of large crowds. First the condemned was drawn: tied to a rope and dragged by a horse to the site of execution. Then he would usually be hung, though often not to the point of death, and once cut down he would be disembowelled and finally dismembered. This last step usually involved tying each limb to a different horse and then setting the beasts off in different directions, thus pulling the condemned person apart. The Welsh Prince Dafydd ap Gruffudd was killed in this way, as was the Scottish patriot William Wallace. Only men found guilty of treason were punished in this way; women would be burnt at the stake for the offence, since it was considered indecent to expose a woman's body to this sort of treatment.

Throughout history this terrible punishment was carried out many times, but by the seventeenth century it had declined. Following Charles II's restoration to the throne there was a spate of such executions. A Bill was passed in Parliament that promised amnesty to all those who had fought against the Crown in the Civil War, but there were exceptions: all those who had been involved in the execution of Charles I were to face a terrible vengeance. Fifty-nine men had signed the King's death warrant, and those who were not dead and who had not fled were rounded up and tried for treason. Those found guilty were to be hung, drawn and quartered and the executioners received instructions that the full horror of the sentence was to be carried out.

Major General Thomas Harrison was the first to be executed, and Samuel Pepys recorded some of the details in his famous diaries. 'I went out to Charing Cross to see Major-General Harrison hanged, drawn and quartered – which was done there – he looked as cheerfully as any man could do in that condition. He was presently cut down and his heart and head shown to people, at which there were great shouts of joy.' Harrison was only allowed to hang for a few seconds before being cut down and disembowelled. He was fully conscious during the whole procedure. At one point while the executioner was rummaging about in his stomach, Harrison sat up and struck him round the head, before dying, screaming in agony.

By the time of the 1715 Scottish uprising, in which many were hung, drawn and quartered, it became usual for the condemned to be hung until they were dead before the disembowelling and quartering proceeded, but it would be another century before the last sentence of hanging, drawing and quartering was pronounced. After the Newport Rising in 1839, when 10,000 Chartists fought pitched battles with the army on the streets of Newport in South Wales, the three men seen as ringleaders were charged with high treason. All were sentenced to be hung, drawn and quartered, but following extensive lobbying of the government in London their sentences were commuted to transportation to Australia. Hanging, drawing and quartering was finally abolished by the Forfeiture Act of 1870.

Chapter Three

The Bloody Code: The Rise of British Hanging

The eighteenth century saw a sea change in the British way of life, as industrialisation started to replace farming. Large numbers of people moved from the countryside, as those who had formerly worked in agriculture sought employment in cities. Some found it difficult to adjust to the new urban society that was being created at breath-taking speed around them. Many were poor, often destitute, and inevitably many would turn to crime to survive. Records from the period show a rise in the number of pickpockets operating in London, as well as housebreakings and armed hold-ups on the streets. It was the same story across the country and the response of the authorities was to instil fear into the hearts of lawbreakers. During the early part of the century there were more than 100 capital offences, many of them unbelievably trivial, and by 1815 this had risen to over 200. This huge expansion of the death penalty came to be known as the Bloody Code, and for the best part of a century it was believed to be the best method of maintaining law and order.

What sort of offences merited hanging under the Bloody Code? Damaging Westminster Bridge was one, engaging in acts of male homosexuality was another, as was stealing from a rabbit warren and impersonating a Chelsea Pensioner. All of these offences could theoretically be met with the death penalty. While it was thought that ferocious laws would reduce crime, this was not what happened at all. There were many reasons for this. Firstly, during the eighteenth and early nineteenth century when the Bloody Code held sway, it was unlikely that one would be caught for any sort of crime. There were no police forces to speak of and no detectives at all. If you were not caught red-handed committing a crime then it was extremely unlikely that you would ever be caught at all. Also with regular public hangings, the public had become hardened to the sight of death. Public executions, intended to be solemn occasions, had taken on a carnival-like atmosphere. The hangings at Tyburn, which took place eight times a year, on the first Monday of the month, came to be known as the Tyburn Fair. Hanging days came to be seen as a kind of holiday. Apprentices were given a day off to attend. There would be a procession in which the condemned would be led from Newgate Prison to the gallows. This was a distance of 3 miles, but it would often take hours. Some of the condemned would be shaking with terror, but there are records that many were in good spirits, joyous even, and exchanged banter with the crowds lining the route. At Tyburn itself stands were set up which, for a price, would give a better view, and nearby homes rented out rooms that had windows overlooking the gallows. Drinks would be sold, as was food and souvenirs, including printed confessions. Today, the site of Tyburn gallows is marked by a plaque on the traffic island between Marble Arch and Edgware Road in London.

The Bloody Code did not, as was intended, bring respect for the law, but rather it brought it into disrepute. Because the law was so harsh, particularly for trifling offences, juries became reluctant to convict. During 1715 for instance more than half of the women on trial for their lives in London were acquitted, and many of those who were found guilty escaped the death penalty because of what became to be known as 'Pious Perjury'. If, for instance, the accused had been found guilty of shoplifting goods worth £2 then this would entail a mandatory death sentence, and so the jury would often find the prisoner guilty of stealing a lesser amount. This sort of dishonesty by juries, although understandable, made a mockery of the law, and resulted in not only criminals but law-abiding people viewing the laws of the country with contempt.

Now we will follow the path from Newgate Prison to Tyburn. On the Sunday before the execution, the condemned men or women would attend chapel where they would spend time atoning for their sins. That night, their last, they would wait alone in their cell contemplating their fate. At midnight the bell in the tower of St Sepulchre Church would sound out and this would be followed by a man ringing a hand bell outside the condemned cells. The man would then recite the following:

> *After you in the condemned hole do lie,*
> *Prepare you, for tomorrow you shall die.*
> *Watch all and pray, the hour is drawing near,*
> *That you before the Almighty must appear.*
> *Examine well yourselves, in times repent,*
> *That you may not to eternal flames be sent.*
> *And when St Sepulchre's bell in the morning tolls,*
> *The Lord above have mercy on your souls.*

In the morning the condemned were taken to the press room to have their chains struck off, and then their arms were tied to their bodies at their elbows. Then they would be placed into a horse-drawn cart for the journey to the gallows. A coffin would be placed in the cart with them, and a noose placed around their necks. Before they left the prison the man with the hand bell would appear again and read out the following speech:

> *All good people, pray heartily unto God for those poor sinners who are going to their death, for whom the great bell doth toll. You that are condemned to die, repent with lamentable tears: ask mercy of the Lord for the salvation of your souls through the merits, death and passion of Jesus Christ, who now sits at the right hand of God, to make intercession for you to return unto him. Lord have mercy upon your soul. Christ have mercy upon you.*

The cart, accompanied by an escort of soldiers, now set off for Tyburn and the gallows. The journey would take several hours as there were a number of stops to be made, most notably at inns and alehouses. Many of these would provide free drinks to condemned men and women on their way to their execution. One of these inns was at St. Giles, where Tottenham Court Road tube station now stands, and here drinks would be dispensed to the condemned and to the crowds following the procession. By the time the procession reached the gallows the condemned could be quite drunk.

Scenes such as this would be played out not only at Tyburn but all over the country. Prisons were generally situated near the centre of towns and the gallows would be on the outskirts, which meant a journey from prison to gallows; part of the entertainment for the gathered crowds. If the crimes were considered awful, the crowds could turn ugly and the condemned would be pelted with mud, stones and even worse as they went on their way to their final fate.

When the procession reached Tyburn, it was to an atmosphere similar to a village fete. Food and drink were on sale, hawkers sold souvenirs, pickpockets worked the crowd beneath the very shadow of the gallows, and grandstands were full of those who had come to watch the show. Before the sentences were carried out the condemned would be given the opportunity to make a speech, and if someone dragged out their speech too long they would be met with scorn from the crowd who were filled with a bloodlust that must have been terrible to behold. People had come to watch someone die not to listen to tedious speeches. Public hangings had become a great attraction, and this was not what the authorities had in mind. Many years after public hangings had ceased at Tyburn, Charles Dickens wrote a letter to *The Times* in which he described a public hanging he had observed. (see plates)

The Criminal Law Consolidation Act of 1861 would reduce the number of capital crimes to just four, thus seeing off the so-called Bloody Code. These were murder, high treason, piracy and arson in a royal dockyard, although in reality no one had been hanged for anything other than murder since 1837. Later in 1864 a Royal Commission looked at capital punishment and while it could see no reason for the abolition of the death penalty, it recommended that public hangings be discontinued. There were further public hangings after the commission but numbers were dwindling. The last public execution in Wales took place in 1866 when John Coe was hanged outside Cardiff prison, while England and Scotland carried out their last public executions in 1868.

On 29 May of that year, the Capital Punishment Amendment Act came into force and public hangings were removed from law. From then on all hangings would take place within prison walls. However, the act neglected to consider the Channel Islands, and on 12 August 1875 Joseph Le Brun was executed in public at St. Helier for the murder of his sister, Nancy. It would not be until 1907 that the law in Jersey finally fell into line with the rest of Britain.

Timeline of British Justice

> 1166 – Henry II re-establishes the system by which royal justices travel the country hearing cases and ensuring that justice is carried out. It is established that sheriffs and county justices have to investigate murders and robberies.

> 1194 – The Eyre Act establishes coroners in England with a jury to look into sudden or unnatural deaths and decide if a crime has occurred.

> 1215 – Trial by jury becomes the norm after the Church withdraws from the system of trial by ordeal. This now means that local men likely to know the circumstances of a crime are able to decide on the veracity of a case.

> 1361 – Justices of the Peace are created in an act that established an office responsible for keeping the King's peace. The magistracy becomes a key element in the administration of criminal justice in the counties.

1624 – A new act to prevent child murder (infanticide) is introduced. This meant that if a mother gave birth alone and the baby died then she was considered guilty of murder. The burden of proof was on the mother to prove that a child was stillborn. This law only applied to unmarried mothers.

1688 – The death penalty is extended to include more than fifty crimes.

1723 – The death sentence is extended once more to include even more crimes. The death penalty can now be handed out for offences such as poaching, arson, maiming of animals and being caught in a forest wearing any sort of disguise.

1724 – The notorious thief Jack Shepard was hanged before a vast crowd at Tyburn. Shepard had previously escaped from gaol four times and he had a following amongst the poor so it was hoped that his execution would act as a deterrent to others.

1777 – Prominent prison reformer John Howard demonstrates concern about the state of prisons and launches a campaign that influences both political leaders and public opinion.

1803 – The infanticide laws are given an overhaul and now the same rules of evidence are followed as in all murder cases. Juries had been reluctant to convict for infanticide since it was a capital offence. The alternative offence of concealment of birth is introduced, with a maximum two-year prison sentence.

1832 – The Abolition of the Punishment of Death Act does away with the Bloody Code and by the late 1840s only the offences of murder and crimes against the state are punishable by death.

1868 – Public executions are outlawed due to the Capital Punishment Amendment Act. All hangings are now to take place in private behind prison walls, although journalists are allowed in as public witnesses.

1953 – John Christie is hanged for the murders of at least eight people. Controversy follows because an innocent man, Timothy Evans, had been hanged for a murder almost certainly committed by Christie.

1955 – The hanging of Ruth Ellis for the murder of her abusive boyfriend David Blakely helps sway public opinion to the side of the abolitionists.

1957 – The Homicide Act limits the death penalty to only certain kinds of murder.

1965 – The Abolition of the Death Penalty Act suspends the the death penalty for five years. In 1969 this is made permanent.

Chapter Four

The Decline of the Death Penalty

Capital punishment would eventually end in Britain not because there was any great feeling on the part of the general public, but rather because liberal and progressive thinkers saw hanging as being out of place with the modern world. But it is a safe bet that if a referendum on the death penalty were held today, a large number of people would support its reintroduction for certain crimes. A YouGov poll in January 2018 found that 54 per cent of members of the Conservative Party supported the return of the death penalty for the most serious crimes, and in November 2018 the Conservative MP John Hayes said there should be a debate to restore capital punishments: 'I say capital punishment should be available to the courts but the death penalty should not be mandatory – that's always been my position' (John Hayes speaking to *Radio Lincolnshire Live*).

During the nineteenth century there were many people who expressed a revulsion for capital punishment. In 1886 the government was growing concerned at the number of botched hangings that were being reported in the newspapers: lurid stories of heads being torn off and prisoners slowly choking to death were commonplace. The Conservative Home Secretary Sir Richard Assheton Cross commissioned a committee to reassess capital punishment, specifically hanging, which in fact was the only form of the death penalty still practised. Known as the Aberdare Committee, after Henry Bruce, the Right Honourable Lord Aberdare who chaired the committee, the brief was to look at the entire process of hanging and later report to the government. The findings of the committee resulted in an official table of drops, which was used to calculate the length of rope for hangings. These recommendations were intended to make the business of hanging more humane: quicker and less prone to mishap.

The committee's report provides a candid insight into the process of hanging in England and Wales between 1868 and 1888. At the start of this period there was no standard gallows, no typical noose, no pinioning method and no real guidelines to a length of drop that would result in instant unconsciousness. Nor was there any uniformity of equipment used in executions. The gallows used would be provided by the county in which the execution took place, and while some were reasonably fit for purpose, others were not. Many were set up in the open air, some required the prisoner to climb a flight of steps to reach the platform. Some gallows had a ring or hook attached to the beam which required the rope to be tied to it with a knot that could slip or tighten, thus altering the drop. The trap doors on which the condemned would stand before execution were sometimes single, sometimes double, and their designs differed widely.

The committee noted that from 1878 the execution rope of standard pattern was used. This 'Government rope', as it was known, was made by John Edgington & Co Ltd of 48 Long Lane, London, and was formed from a 10 foot 2½ inch length of ¾ inch diameter Italian hemp with a metal eyelet for the noose. The rope would be ordered from Newgate prison by the officials of the county requiring it. Before 1878 hangmen had supplied their own ropes, but this was not considered satisfactory. Nor was their propensity for showing off and indeed selling off used ropes for profit. The committee would recommend that only government issued ropes be used for all future executions.

A year into their study, the commission took evidence from hangman James Berry, which included a discussion into the elasticity of the ropes supplied by the prison office. The elasticity issue was important because if the rope stretched the condemned got a greater drop, but if there was no elasticity there was an increased chance of decapitation.

There was also discussion of the correct position for the eyelet or thimble of the noose, and Berry was of the view that it should be placed behind the left ear, the 'sub-aural' position. Berry would later become unpopular with the Home Office because of his holding court in local pubs after executions. Questions were asked in Parliament, and Berry was replaced as the government's chief hangman by James Billington. Berry though had put together his own table for calculating the scale of drops for hangings and the committee were interested in this; they would later use it to produce their own official table of drops.

Berry had carried out 131 hangings during his time as official hangman. These included five women, and perhaps that of the notorious serial killer Jack the Ripper. In 1889 Berry had hung William Henry Bury for the murder of his wife and it was only later that it became apparent that Bury had been one of the many suspects in the Whitechapel murders of 1888. When Berry published his memoirs in *Thomson's Weekly News* of 12 February 1927, the former hangman stated that he believed Bury and the Whitechapel killer to have been one and the same.

William Henry Bury was hanged for the murder of his wife Ellen, a former prostitute, in 1889. He had murdered his wife shortly after the height of the Whitechapel murders, and similarities between the murder of his wife and the infamous series of killings led the press to speculate that Bury had been the Ripper. This was not the view of the police, but the newspapers, then as now, would not let the facts get in the way of a good story. More likely to have been the Ripper was George Chapman, hanged in April 1903: his story is detailed later in this book.

The Aberdare Committee reported in July 1888, and although no further legislation was made, most of the committee's suggestions were implemented by the government. It was decided to recommend a striking force of 1,260 ft. lbs. except for very light prisoners where an energy of 1,120 ft. lbs. was deemed sufficient.

The Aberdare report gave the first national execution protocol and many of its recommendations would continue to be used up to the abolition of the death penalty.

After the Second World War the movement for the abolition of the death penalty stepped up a gear. In 1948 the Labour MP Sidney Silverman introduced a private member's bill calling for the suspension of the death penalty for five years. This was passed by the Commons but rejected by the Lords.

Later that year a Royal Commission was set up under Sir Ernest Gowers to examine the death penalty in Britain. The commission published their findings five years later, and although it did not call for the abolition of the death penalty, there were concerns expressed at the mental health of many of those tried for murder. Perhaps the most striking part of the report was that it believed the death penalty was not a deterrent to murder. Since this was the main justification for hanging people, it gave great strength to the abolitionists who were growing ever more vocal in their opposition to capital punishment.

The following decade saw several high-profile cases that caused unease about the way the death penalty was being carried out. The case of Derek Bentley was one – more about him later.

Another was that of Timothy Evans. In 1953 John Christie, a serial strangler of women, was tried and executed. But during Christie's trial it emerged that his one-time lodger, a feeble-minded Welshman named Timothy Evans, had been arrested for strangling his wife and daughter in 1950 (though he was only tried and convicted of the murder of his daughter).

During the 1950s the hanging of women inspired much unfavourable attention on the death penalty. There were three women hanged during that decade, the most famous being the 1955 execution of Ruth Ellis that provoked widespread protests. These cases will be dealt with in detail in a later section of this book.

Sidney Silverman again introduced a bill to abolish hanging in 1955, and the Home Secretary announced that there would be no more hangings until the will of Parliament was known. The Bill went through Parliament with a majority, but once again the Lords threw it out.

Labour fought the 1964 General Election with a manifesto committed to the abolition of the death penalty. It was clear by this time that hanging was coming to an end even without legislation. In 1902 there had been twenty-nine hangings across England and Wales, and by 1951 this had dwindled to fifteen. The Labour Party won the 1964 election and Prime Minister Harold Wilson made it clear that the abolition of the death penalty was a priority. A year later Sidney Silverman introduced another private member's bill for the abolition of the death penalty, and the Home Secretary commuted all sentences of death which had been passed since October 1964. On 28 October 1965 Silverman's bill received Royal Consent and the death penalty was suspended for five years. Then, in December 1969, a free vote was held in the Commons which finally endorsed the abolition of hanging for murder. The vote was 343 in favour of abolition and 185 against.

In theory the death penalty remained for certain crimes, and it wasn't until 1971, with the implementation of the Criminal Damage Act, that arson in the Royal Dockyards ceased to be a capital offence. The death penalty remained with the civil courts for treason and piracy and the military courts could impose it during times of war for certain offences. In 1973 the death penalty was abolished in Northern Ireland.

There were still those who fought for the death penalty to be restored and in 1988 the Commons held another free vote on the restoration of capital punishment. Prime Minister Margaret Thatcher was in favour of restoring the death penalty, but the House voted 341 to 218 against. Two years later there was another vote, though this time there was an even greater majority against restoration.

The true formal and irrevocable end of the death penalty in Britain passed almost without comment towards the end of the millennium. In 1998 the Crime and Disorder Bill abolished the death penalty for treason and piracy, and that same year Parliament voted to ratify the sixth protocol of the European Convention on Human Rights, which prohibits the use of the death penalty except in times of war. This final step absolutely prohibits the use of capital punishment as long as Britain remains in the European Union.

Chapter Five

Judicial Executions 1900-10

In the first decade of the new century the number of executions were:

1900	14
1901	16
1902	23
1903	27
1904	19
1905	18
1906	8
1907	11
1908	15
1909	21
1910	16

1900

Louisa Josephine Jemima Masset, age 33, convicted of the murder of 3-year-old Manfred Lois Masset. Executed at Newgate, 9 January 1900. Hangman: James Billington.

Ada Chard-Williams, age 24, convicted of the murder of 21-month-old Selina Helen Jones. Executed at Newgate, 6 March 1900. Hangman: James Billington.

Although Ada Chard-Williams was tried and convicted of only one murder, she was probably responsible for others. She was a 'baby farmer': for a fee she would supposedly help out young mothers who could not care for their children by finding loving homes for them. The truth was that these children would simply disappear, more often than not never heard of again.

Henry Grove, age 26, convicted of the murder of Henry Smith. Executed at Newgate, 22 May 1900. Hangman: James Billington.

Alfred Highfield, age 22, convicted of the murder of fiancée Edith Margaret Poole. Executed at Newgate, 17 July 1900. Hangman: James Billington.

William James Irwin, age 61, convicted of the murder of wife Catherine Amelia. Executed at Newgate, 14 August 1900. Hangman: James Billington.

Charles Benjamin Backhouse, age 23, convicted of the murder of PC John William Kew. Executed at Leeds, 16 August 1900. Hangman: James Billington.

Thomas Mellor, age 29, convicted of the murder of his daughter Ada Beecroft. Executed at Leeds, 16 August 1900. Hangman: James Billington.
    On the night of 11 May 1900, Thomas Mellor killed both his illegitimate daughters, Ada aged 6 and Annie aged 4, by drowning them in the Leeds/ Liverpool canal. It was then usual in British law for murderers to only be prosecuted for the one killing and at his trial evidence was only given regarding Ada's murder. Mellor was therefore convicted and hanged for the murder of the older sister only.

William Lacey, age 29, convicted of the murder of girlfriend Pauline Lacey. Executed at Cardiff Prison, 21 August 1900. Hangman: James Billington. See *Dark Valleys: Foul Deeds Among the South Wales Valleys 1845–2016* (Pen and Sword, 2016).

Charles Oliver Blewitt, age 33, convicted of the murder of wife Mary Ann. Executed at Leeds, 28 August 1900. Hangman: James Billington.

John Charles Parr, age 19, convicted of the murder of girlfriend Sarah Willett. Executed at Newgate, 2 October 1900. Hangman: James Billington.

William Burrett, age 35, convicted of the murder of wife Ada Grubb Burrett. Executed at Chelmsford, 3 October 1900. Hangman: James Billington.

Joseph Holden, age 57, convicted of the murder of John Dawes. Executed at Manchester, 4 December 1900. Hangman: James Billington.

John Bowes, age 50, convicted of the murder of his wife Isabella. Executed at Durham, 12 December 1900. Hangman: James Billington.

James Joseph Bergin, age 28, convicted of the murder of his fiancée Margaret Morrison. Executed at Liverpool, 27 December 1900. Hangman: James Billington.

1901

William Woods, age 58, convicted of the murder of girlfriend Bridget McGivern. Executed at Belfast, 11 January 1901. Hangman: Thomas Scott.

Samson Silas Salmon, age 32, convicted of the murder of Lucy Smith. Executed at Newgate, 19 February 1901. Hangman: James Billington.

George Henry Parker, age 23, convicted of the murder of William Pearson. Executed at Wandsworth, 2 March 1901. Hangman: James Billington.

Herbert John Bennett, age 22, convicted of the murder of his wife Mary Jane. Executed at Norwich, 21 March 1901. Hangman: James Billington.

Joseph Arthur Shufflebotham, age 38, convicted of the murder of wife Elizabeth. Executed at Stafford, 2 April 1901. Hangman: James Billington.

Valeri Giovanni, age 31, convicted of the murder of Victor Baileff. Executed at Bodmin, 17 June 1901. Hangman: James Billington.

Charles Richard Thomas Watkins, age 54, convicted of the murder of Frederick William Acland Hamilton. Executed at Maidstone, 12 July 1901. Hangman: James Billington.

Ernest Walter Wickham, age 30, convicted of the murder of girlfriend Amy Eugenie Russell. Executed at Wandsworth, 23 July 1901. Hangman: James Billington.

John Joyce, age 36, convicted of the murder of John Nugent. Executed at Birmingham, 31 July 1901. Hangman: James Billington.

Marcel Fougeron, age 23, convicted of the murder of Hermann Francis Jung. Executed at Newgate, 19 November 1901. Hangman: James Billington.

Patrick Mckenna, age 53, convicted of the murder of wife Anna. Executed at Manchester, 3 December 1901. Hangman: James Billington.

John and Robert Miller, aged 67 and 31, jointly convicted of the murder of John Ferguson. Executed at Newcastle, 7 December 1901. Hangman: William Billington.

John George Thompson, age 38, convicted of the murder of girlfriend Maggie Ann Lieutand. Executed at Durham, 10 December 1901. Hangman: William Billington.

Alexander Claydon, age 43, convicted of the murder of wife Louisa. Executed at Northampton, 13 December 1901. Hangman: William Billington.

John Harrison, age 31, convicted of the murder of wife Alice Ann. Executed at Liverpool, 2 December 1901. Hangman: William Billington.

1902

Harold Amos Apted, age 20, convicted of the murder of Frances Eliza O'Rourke. Executed at Maidstone, 15 March 1902. Hangman: William Billington.
    In this particularly horrendous crime, 7-year-old Frances was abducted, raped and murdered before being thrown into Vauxhall Pond near Tonbridge Wells.

Richard Wigley, age 34, convicted of the murder of girlfriend Mary Ellen Bowen. Executed at Shrewsbury, 18 March 1902. Hangman: Henry Pierrepoint.

Arthur Richardson, age 20, convicted of the murder of Sara Hebden. Executed at Hull, 6 March 1902. Hangman: William Billington.

Charles Robert Earl, age 56, convicted of the murder of Margaret Pamphilon. Executed at Wandsworth, 29 April 1902. Hangman: Henry Pierrepoint.

George Woolfe, age 21, convicted of the murder of his girlfriend Charlotte Cheeseman. Executed at Newgate, 6 May 1902. Hangman: William Billington.

George Woolfe would enter the history books as the last man to be hanged at Newgate.

Thomas Marsland, age 21, convicted of the murder of wife Elizabeth. Executed at Liverpool, 20 May 1902. Hangman: William Billington.

Samuel Middleton, age 46, convicted of the murder of wife Hannah. Executed at Worcester, 15 July 1902. Hangman: William Billington.

William Churcher, age 35, convicted of the murder of Sophia Jane Hepworth. Executed at Winchester, 2 July 1902. Hangman: William Billington.
    William Churcher stabbed his girlfriend, 30-year-old Sophia Hepworth, thirty-three times in a frenzied attack.

John Bedford, age 41, convicted of the murder of girlfriend Nancy Price. Executed at Derby, 30 July 1902. Hangman: Henry Pierrepoint.

William Lane, age 47, convicted of the murder of Elizabeth Dyson. Executed at Stafford, 12 August 1902. Hangman: William Billington.
    William Lane had spent twelve years as a policeman in Bradford and knew full well the consequences of murder. When he cut the throat of his girlfriend, a woman twenty years older than he was, he said that it had been a suicide pact. He claimed that she had asked him to cut her throat, and that he had intended to bring the blade to his own throat but was unable to do so. A jury found him guilty of murder and instead a rope was taken to his throat.

George William Hibbs, age 40, convicted of the murder of his landlady Mariam Jane Tye. Executed at Wandsworth, 13 August 1902. Hangman: William Billington.

John MacDonald, age 24, convicted of the murder of Henry Groves. Executed at Pentonville, 30 September 1902. Hangman: William Billington.
    'I did it and that is the knife I did it with', MacDonald told the police after his arrest for murdering Henry Groves at a Salvation Army shelter they had both been using. He would become the first man to be hanged at Pentonville.

Henry Williams, age 31, convicted of the murder of daughter Margaret Anne Andrews. Executed at Pentonville, 11 November 1902. Hangman: William Billington.

The case surrounding Henry Williams, a veteran of the Boer War, is particularly sad. Before leaving for military service he had been in a relationship with Ellen Andrews, a widow. They had a child they named Margaret Anne, and by all accounts Henry doted on her. By the time Henry returned from active service his daughter was 5 years old, and Henry was a changed man: nowadays he would be diagnosed as suffering from stress. He became convinced that Ellen had been seeing other men while he had been away and there were many rows, resulting in them separating.

On 10 September 1902, Henry brought his daughter to stay in London with him. He put her to bed and told her they were going to play a game. He then placed a hand over her eyes and cut her throat with a razor. He was a broken man afterwards and didn't want to live. He confessed his crime to the police, was arrested and said not a word as he was led to the gallows.

Patrick Leggett, age 30, convicted of the murder of wife Sarah Jane. Executed at Glasgow, 22 October 1902. Hangman: William Billington.

Henry McWiggins, age 29, convicted of the murder of common-law wife Esther Bedford. Executed at Manchester, 2 December 1902. Hangman: William Billington.

William Chambers, age 47, convicted of the murders of wife Emily Chambers and mother-in-law Mary Oakley. Executed at Bedford, 4 December 1902. Hangman: William Billington.

Thomas Fairclough Barrow, age 49, convicted of the murder of common-law-wife Emily Coates. Executed at Pentonville, 9 December 1902. Hangman: William Billington.

Jeremiah Callaghan, age 42, convicted of the murder of girlfriend Hannah Shea. Executed at Usk, 12 December 1902. Hangman: William Billington.

Samuel Thomas Walton, age 31, convicted of the murders of wife Isabela, daughter Nora, and mother-in-law Mrs Young. Executed at Durham, 16 December 1902. Hangman: William Billington.

Thomas Nicholson, age 24, convicted of the murder of Mary Ina Stewart. Executed at Durham, 16 December 1902. Hangman: William Billington.

William Brown, age 42, convicted of the murder of wife Elizabeth. Executed at Wandsworth, 16 December 1902. Hangman: Henry Pierrepoint.

William James Bolton, age 44, convicted of the murder of girlfriend Jane Elizabeth Allen. Executed at Hull, 23 December 1902. Hangman: William Billington.

George Place, age 28, convicted of the murders of Eliza Chetwynd and an unnamed child. Executed at Warwick, 30 December 1902. Hangman: Henry Pierrepoint.

1903

Amelia Sach and Annie Walters, age 29 and 54, jointly convicted of the murder of a male infant. Executed at Holloway, 3 February 1903. Hangman: William Billington.

Police were suspicious of what was going on in Claymore House, East Finchley, an establishment operating as a nursing home for unmarried mothers, and in November of 1902 they followed Annie Walters when she left the establishment carrying a small bundle. The woman was stopped and it was discovered that the package she had been carrying contained the body of a baby. The police then arrested Amelia Sach, who actually owned the house in East Finchley. The two women became known as the Finchley Baby Killers and police suspected that their baby farming service was responsible for many of the tiny corpses turning up around London.

The two women had advertised their service to unmarried mothers in several newspapers. They would, the adverts claimed, help with the delivery and afterwards find suitable foster homes for the unwanted children. They received a handsome fee for this. The service, known as baby farming, was illegal at that time, and indeed was seen by many as a valuable, even charitable, public service, since the unfortunate women giving birth were often alone and had no way of caring for a new child. Murder though was illegal and if finding homes proved difficult, Annie Walters would inject the infants with chlorodyne, a morphine-based drug, and the baby would die from asphyxia.

On 3 March 1903, a month after the two women had been executed, *The Evening Bulletin* ran a story that claimed that in the time leading up to the arrest of the two women, police had been finding the bodies of babies, around 100 a year, all across London, and that since the two women faced justice the number of tiny corpses had dropped considerably. There could, the newspaper claimed, be only one inference: that a large number of these little corpses came from the Finchley baby farm.

The two women were convicted of killing only the one child, but police did believe that the pair were responsible for several dozen deaths.

William Hughes, age 42, convicted of the murder of wife Jane Hannah. Executed at Ruthin, 17 February 1903. Hangman: William Billington.

Edgar Edwards, age 44, convicted of the murder of John, Beatrice and Ethel Darby. Executed at Wandsworth, 3 March 1903. Hangman: William Billington.

Samuel Henry Smith, age 45, convicted of the murder of girlfriend Lucy Lingard. Executed at Lincoln, 10 March 1903. Hangman: William Billington.

George Chapman, age 37, convicted of the murders of Isabella Mary Spink, Elizabeth Taylor and Maud Marsh. Executed at Wandsworth, 7 April 1903. Hangman: William Billington.

George Chapman, real name Severin Kiosowski, was a Polish immigrant who changed his name to George Chapman shortly after arriving in London in 1888. In 1903, when he was tried and convicted of poisoning three women, all of whom he had had relationships with, he became known as the Borough Poisoner, but there were strong suspicions that he was actually Jack the Ripper. Inspector Abberline, the man who had led the Ripper investigation, was convinced that George Chapman and the Ripper were one and the same, and when Chapman was arrested, Abberline was reported to have said, 'I see you've got Jack the Ripper at last.'

The truth will probably never be known but Chapman remains a strong suspect. If he was Jack the Ripper, then in 1903 he took the secret to his grave.

William John Hudson, age 26, convicted of the murder of Harry Short. Executed at Manchester, 12 May 1903. Hangman: William Billington.

Gustav Rau and Willem Schmidt, ages 28 and 30, convicted of the murders of Alexander Mcleaod, Julius Herrison, Patrick Durran, Fred Abrahamson, Captain Alexander Shaw, Gustav Johanson and Alexander Bravo. Executed at Liverpool, 2 June 1903. Hangman: William Billington.

The hanging of Rau and Schmidt was the first double hanging to take place at Woolton prison. The two men had been found guilty of leading a mutiny on board the SS *Veronica* in which the ship's captain and several crew members were murdered.

Charles Howell, age 30, convicted of the murder of girlfriend Maud Luen. Executed at Chelmsford, 7 July 1903. Hangman: William Billington.

Samuel Herbert Dougal, age 57, convicted of the murder of girlfriend Camille Cecile Holland. Executed at Chelmsford, 14 July 1903. Hangman: William Billington.

Thomas Porter and Thomas Preston, aged 29 and 24, convicted jointly of the murder of Constable William Wilkinson. Executed at Leicester, 21 July 1903. Hangman: William Billington.

Leonard Pachett, age 26, convicted of the murder of wife Sarah Ann. Executed at Lincoln, 28 July 1903. Hangman: William Billington.

Charles Jeremiah Slowe, age 28, convicted of the murder of Martha Jane Hardwick. Executed at Pentonville, 21 October 1903. Hangman: William Billington.

Edward Richard Palmer, age 24, convicted of the murder of fiancée, Esther Swinford. Executed at Devizes, 17 November 1903. Hangman: William Billington.

Bernard White, age 21, convicted of the murder of girlfriend Maud Garrett. Executed at Chelmsford, 1 December 1903. Hangman: William Billington.

Charles Wood Whittaker, age 43, convicted of the murder of mistress Eliza Range. Executed at Manchester, 2 December 1903. Hangman: William Billington.

James Duffy, age 46, convicted of the murder of girlfriend Ellen Newman. Executed at Durham, 8 December 1903. Hangman: William Billington.

William Haywood, age 61, convicted of the murder of wife Jane. Executed at Hereford, 16 December 1903. Hangman: Henry Pierrepoint.

William Brown and Thomas Cowdrey, aged 27 and 36, jointly convicted of the murder of Esther Atkins. Executed at Winchester, 16 December 1903.

Charles William Ashton, age 19, convicted of the murder of girlfriend Annie Marshall. Executed at Hull, 22 December 1903. Hangman: William Billington.

John Gallagher and Emily Swann, aged 30 and 42, jointly convicted of the murder of William Swann. Executed at Leeds, 29 December 1903. Hangman: William Billington.

Henry Bertram Starr, age 31, convicted of the murder of wife Mary. Executed at Liverpool, 29 December 1903. Hangman: James Billington.

1904

Joseph Moran, age 26, convicted of the rape and murder of Rose Ann McCann. Executed at Londonderry, 5 January 1904. Hangman: William Billington.

Sidney George Smith, age 23, convicted of the murder of girlfriend Alice Woodman. Executed at Gloucester, 15 February 1904. Hangman: William Billington.

James Henry Clarkson, age 19, convicted of the murder of Elizabeth Mary Lynas. Executed at Leeds, 8 March 1904. Hangman: William Billington.

Henry Jones, age 50, convicted of the murder of girlfriend Mary Gilbert. Executed at Stafford, 29 March 1904. hangmen was John Billington.

Charles Samuel Dyer, Age 25, convicted of the murder of girlfriend Martha Eliza Simpson. Executed at Birmingham, 5 April 1904. Hangman: William Billington.

William Kirwan, age 39, convicted of the murder of sister-in-law Mary Pike. Executed at Liverpool, 31 May 1904. Hangman: William Billington.

Ping Lun, age 43, convicted of the murder of John Go Hing. Executed at Liverpool, 31 May 1904. Hangman: William Billington.
    There was a disturbance at the execution of the Chinaman when the hangman walked into his cell and said, 'Come on Ping Pong'. The racist remark from William Billington sent Ping Lun into a frenzy and he had to be dragged to the scaffold by several prison officers.

John Sullivan, age 40, convicted of the murder of Dennis Lowthian. Executed at Pentonville, 12 July 1904. Hangman: William Billington.

Samuel Rowledge, age 37, convicted of the murder of girlfriend Alice Foster. Executed at Northampton, 13 July 1904. Hangman: William Billington.

Thomas Gunning, age 48, convicted of the murder of common-law wife Agnes Allen. Executed at Glasgow, 26 July 1904. Hangman: William Billington.

George Breeze, age 21, convicted of the murder of Margaret Jane Chisholm. Executed at Durham, 2 August 1904. Hangman: William Billington.

John Thomas Kay, age 52, convicted of the murder of girlfriend Jane Hirst. Executed at Leeds, 16 August 1904. Hangman: John Billington.

Samuel Holden, age 43, convicted of the murder of girlfriend Susan Humphries. Executed at Birmingham, 16 August 1904. Hangman: William Billington.

Joseph Potter and Charles Wade, aged 35 and 22, convicted jointly of the murder of Matilda Emily Farmer. Executed at Pentonville, December 13 1904. Hangman: William Billington.

Edmund Hall, age 49, convicted of the murder of father-in-law John Dalby. Executed at Leeds, 20 December 1904. Hangman: John Billington.

Eric Lange, age 30, convicted of the murder of John Emlyn Jones. Executed at Cardiff, 21 December 1904. Hangman: William Billington.
    See *Dark Valleys* (Pen and Sword, 2016).

Joseph Fee, age 23, convicted of the murder of John Flanagan. Executed at Armagh, 22 December 1904. Hangman: Henry Pierrepoint.

Arthur Jeffries, age 44, convicted of the murder of Samuel Barker. Executed at Leeds, 29 December 1904. Hangman: John Billington.

1905

Edward Harrison, age 62, convicted of the murder of daughter Elizabeth Rickus. Executed at Wandsworth, 28 February 1905. Hangman: John Billington.

John Hutchinson, age 29, convicted of the murder of Albert Mathews. Executed at Nottingham, 29 March 1905. Hangman: John Billington.

Alfred Bridgeman, age 22, convicted of the murder of Catherina Balhard. Executed at Pentonville, 26 April 1905. Hangman: John Billington.

Alfred Stratton and Albert Ernest, aged 22 and 20, jointly convicted of the murders of Thomas and Ann Farrow. Executed at Wandsworth, 23 May 1905. Hangman: John Billington.

Thomas Farrow was found dead, brutally beaten to death at his paint store in Deptford, London, on the morning of 24 March 1905; his wife Ann lay in bed upstairs. She too had been battered but was still alive, though would die from her injuries a few days later. The motive had been robbery which led the police to arrest the brothers Alfred and Albert Stratton. Theirs was the first case in Britain in which fingerprint evidence secured their conviction. The victims were aged 69 and 65.

Alfred John Heal, age 22, convicted of the murder of fiancée Ellen Goodspeed. Executed at Wandsworth, 20 June 1905. Hangman: John Billington.

Ferat Mohamed Ben Ali, age 19, convicted of the murder of Hadjou Hidder. Executed at Maidstone, 1 August 1905. Hangman: Henry Pierrepoint.

William Alfred Hancocks, age 35, convicted of the murder of daughter Mary Elizabeth Hancocks. Executed at Knutsford, 9 August 1905. Hangman: John Billington.

Arthur Devereaux, age not recorded in court records, convicted of the murder of wife and daughters: Beatrix, Laurence and Evelyn. Executed at Pentonville, 15 August 1905. Hangman: Henry Pierrepoint.

Thomas George Tattersall, age 31, convicted of the murder of Rebecca Tattersall. Executed at Leeds, 15 August 1905. Hangman: John Billington.

George William Butler, age 50, convicted of the murder of girlfriend Mary Allen. Executed at Pentonville, 7 November 1905. Hangman: Henry Pierrepoint.

Pasha Liffey, age 20, convicted of the murder of Mary Jane Welsh. Executed at Glasgow, 14 November 1905. Hangman: Henry Pierrepoint.

William Yarnold, age 48, convicted of the murder of wife Annie. Executed at Worcester, 5 December 1905. Hangman: Henry Pierrepoint.

Henry Perkins, age 40, convicted of the murder of Patrick Durkin. Executed at Newcastle, 6 December 1905. Hangman: Henry Pierrepoint.

Samuel Curtis, age 60, convicted of the murder of girlfriend Alice Clover. Executed at Maidstone, 20 December 1905. Hangman: Henry Pierrepoint.

Fredrick William Edge, age 23, convicted of the murder of Francis Walter Evans. Executed at Stafford, 27 December 1905. Hangman: Henry Pierrepoint.

George Smith, age 40, convicted of the murder of Martha Smith. Executed at Leeds, 28 December 1905. Hangman: Henry Pierrepoint.

John Silk, age 30, convicted of the murder of mother Mary Fallon. Executed at Derby, 29 December 1905. Hangman: Henry Pierrepoint.

1906

John Griffith, age 19, convicted of the murder of 17-year-old Catherine Garrity. Executed at Manchester, 27 February 1905. Hangman: Henry Pierrepoint.

Was John Griffiths an innocent man who went to the gallows? Catherine was an ex-girlfriend of Griffiths' and he had threatened her several times. She had even taken Griffiths to court over the threats and he had been bound over to keep the peace. Witnesses claimed to have seen Griffiths hanging around the old stables where Catherine's body was found. Police discovered bloodstains on his clothing, and footprints matching the distinctive clogs he wore were also found near the body. It was enough for the jury to bring in a guilty verdict and send Griffiths to the gallows. However, shortly before the execution took place, Catherine Garrity's mother received an anonymous letter, postmarked Ashford in Kent. The letter contained a full confession to the murder of Catherine, which seemed to clear Griffiths of the crime. However the authorities decided not to take the letter seriously and Griffiths went to the gallows.

Harold Walters, age 39, convicted of the murder of girlfriend Sarah Ann McConnell. Executed at Wakefield, 10 April 1906. Hangman: Henry Pierrepoint.

Edward Glyn, age 26, convicted of the murder of girlfriend Jane Gamble. Executed at Nottingham, 7 August 1906. Hangman: Henry Pierrepoint.

Thomas Mouncer, age 25, convicted of the murder of girlfriend Elizabeth Baldwin. Executed at Wakefield, 21 July 1906. Hangman: Henry Pierrepoint.

Fredrick Reynolds, age 23, convicted of the murder of ex-girlfriend Sophia Lovell. Executed at Wandsworth, 13 November 1906. Hangman: Henry Pierrepoint.

Edward Hartigan, age 58, convicted of the murder of wife Catherine. Executed at Knutsford, 27 November 1906. Hangman: Henry Pierrepoint.

Richard Buckham, age 20, convicted of the murder of Albert and Emma Watson. Executed at Chelmsford, 4 December 1906. Hangman: Henry Pierrepoint.

Walter Marsh, age 39, convicted of the murder of wife Eliza. Executed at Derby, 27 December 1906. Hangman: Thomas Pierrepoint.

1907

John Davies, age 53, convicted of the murder of girlfriend Jane Harrison. Executed at Warwick, 1 January 1907. Hangman: John Ellis.

Thomas Connan, age 29, convicted of the murder of brother-in-law Pierre Le Guen. Executed at St. Hellier, Jersey, 19 February 1907. Hangman: Henry Pierrepoint.

Joseph Jones, age 60, convicted of the murder of son-in-law Edmund Clarke. Executed at Stafford, 26 March 1907. Hangman: Henry Pierrepoint.

Edwin James Moore, age 33, convicted of the murder of mother Fanny. Executed at Warwick, 2 April 1907. Hangman: John Ellis.

On the evening of 2 March 1907, Edwin James Moore argued with his mother over his dinner; a trivial matter which ended with tragic consequences. During the fight Moore threw a paraffin lamp at his mother, setting her alight. She would die of horrific burns and Edwin would face the hangman. The victim was 52 years old.

William Edward Slack, age 47, convicted of the murder of Lucy Wilson. Executed at Derby, 16 July 1907. Hangman: Henry Pierrepoint.

Charles Paterson, age 37, convicted of the murder of girlfriend Lillian Charlton. Executed at Liverpool, 7 August 1907. Hangman: Henry Pierrepoint.

Richard Clifford Brinkley, age 53, convicted of the murders of Richard and Elizabeth Beck. Executed at Wandsworth, 13 August 1907. Hangman: Henry Pierrepoint.

Rhoda Willis, age 44, convicted of the murder of an unnamed female child. Executed at Cardiff, 14 August 1907. Hangman: Henry Pierrepoint.

Rhoda Willis was a baby farmer and may have been responsible for the murders of several new-born infants, however she was found guilty of killing only one child, by asphyxiation. The case is an interesting one and the full story can be found in *Dark Valleys* (Pen and Sword, 2016).

William Austin, age 31, convicted of the murder of Unity Annie Butler. Executed at Reading, 5 November 1907. Hangman: Henry Pierrepoint.

William Duddles, age 47, convicted of the murder of Catherine Gear. Executed at Lincoln, 20 November 1907. Hangman: Henry Pierrepoint.

George Stills, age 30, convicted of the murder of mother, Rachel Stills. Executed at Cardiff, 13 December 1907. Hangman: Henry Pierrepoint.

The full story of this case is detailed in *Dark Valleys* (Pen and Sword, 2016).

1908

Joseph Hume, age 25, convicted of the murder of John Barclay Smith. Executed at Inverness, 6 March 1908. Hangman: Henry Pierrepoint.

Joseph William Noble, age 46, convicted of the murder of John Patterson. Executed at Durham, 24 March 1908. Hangman: Thomas Pierrepoint.

Robert Lawman, age 35, convicted of the murder of girlfriend Amelia Bell Wood. Executed at Durham, 24 March 1908. Hangman: Henry Pierrepoint.

John Ramsbottom, age 34, convicted of the murder of brother-in-law James McCraw. Executed at Manchester, 23 April 1908. Hangman: Henry Pierrepoint.

Fredrick Ballington, age 41, convicted of the murder of wife Ellen Ann. Executed at Manchester, 28 July 1908. Hangman: Henry Pierrepoint.

Thomas Siddle, age 29, convicted of the murder of wife Gertrude. Executed at Hull, 4 August 1908. Hangman: Henry Pierrepoint.

Mathew James Dodds, age 44, convicted of the murder of wife Mary Jane. Executed at Durham, 5 August 1908. Hangman: Henry Pierrepoint.

Edward Johnstone, age 32, convicted of the murder of girlfriend Jane Wallace. Executed at Perth, 19 August 1908. Hangman: John Ellis.

John Berryman, age 53, convicted of the murders of brother and sister-in-law, William and Jean Berryman. Executed at Londonderry, 20 August 1908. Hangman: Henry Pierrepoint.

James Phipps, age 21, convicted of the murder of Elizabeth Warburton. Executed at Knutsford, 12 November 1908. Hangman: Henry Pierrepoint.

James Nicholls, age 35, convicted of the murder of Susan Wilson. Executed at Norwich, 2 December 1908. Hangman: Henry Pierrepoint.

John William Ellwood, age 44, convicted of the murder of Thomas Wilkinson. Executed at Leeds, 3 December 1908. Hangman: Henry Pierrepoint.

William Bouldry, age 41, convicted of the murder of wife Margaret. Executed at Maidstone, 8 December 1908. Hangman: Henry Pierrepoint.

Harry Thomas Parker, age 32, convicted of the murder of Thomas Tomkins. Executed at Warwick, 15 December 1908. Hangman: Henry Pierrepoint.

Patrick Collins, age 24, convicted of the murder of Annie Lawrence. Executed at Cardiff, 30 December 1908. Hangman: Henry Pierrepoint.

1909

John Murphy, age 21, convicted of the murder of Julius Schlittle. Executed at Pentonville, 6 January 1909. Hangman: Henry Pierrepoint.

Jeremiah O'Connor, age 52, convicted of the murder of Mary Donnelly. Executed at Durham, 23 February 1909. Hangman: Henry Pierrepoint.

Ernest Hutchinson, age 24, convicted of the murder of Hannah Maria Whitley. Executed at Wakefield, 2 March 1909. Hangman: Henry Pierrepoint.

Thomas Mead, age 33, convicted of the murder of Clara Howell. Executed at Leeds, 12 March 1909. Hangman: Henry Pierrepoint.

Edmund Walter Elliott, age 19, convicted of the murder of Clara Jane Hannaford. Executed at Exeter, 30 March 1909. Hangman: John Ellis.

See Lee, age 38, convicted of the murder of Yun Yap. Executed at Liverpool, 30 March 1909. Hangman: Henry Pierrepoint.

Joseph Edward Jones, age 39, convicted of the murder of wife Charlotte. Executed at Stafford, 13 April 1909. Hangman: Henry Pierrepoint.

William Joseph Foy, age 25, convicted of the murder of girlfriend Mary Ann Rees. Executed at Swansea, 8 May 1909. Hangman: Henry Pierrepoint.
    This case is covered in greater detail in *Dark Valleys* (Pen and Sword, 2016).

Morris and Mark Reuben, aged 23 and 22, convicted jointly of the murder of William Sproull. Executed at Pentonville, 20 May 1909. Hangman: Henry Pierrepoint.

John Edmunds, age 24, convicted of the murder of Cecilia Harris. Executed at Usk, 3 July 1909. Hangman: Henry Pierrepoint.

'Jack Edmunds shot me and cut my throat, he got my money,' said the bloodstained note that 59-year-old Cecilia Harris wrote just before she died. Left for dead by the cold-blooded killer, she had managed to stagger to a nearby farmhouse where she wrote the note that convicted him.

Alexander Edmunstone, age 23, convicted of the murder of Michael Brown. Executed at Perth, 16 July 1909. Hangman: John Ellis.

William Davies, age 37, convicted of the murder of girlfriend Hester Harriet Richards. Executed at Wakefield, 19 July 1909. Hangman: Henry Pierrepoint.

William Hampton, age 23, convicted of the murder of girlfriend Emily Barnes Tredrea. Executed at Bodmin, 20 July 1909. Hangman: Henry Pierrepoint.

Mark Shawcross, age 30, convicted of the murder of girlfriend Emily Ramsbottom. Executed at Manchester, 3 August 1909. Hangman: Henry Pierrepoint.

Julius Wammer, age 43, convicted of the murder of Cissie Archer. Executed at Wandsworth, 10 August 1909. Hangman: Henry Pierrepoint.

Madar Lal Dhingra, age 25, convicted of the murders of Sir William Hutt Curzon-Wylie (Secretary of State for India) and Cawas Lalcaca. Executed at Pentonville, 17 August 1909. Hangman: Henry Pierrepoint.

On 1 July 1909 Madar, a young Indian man, stood outside London's Imperial Institute in South Kensington where a concert had been taking place. He was waiting for Sir William Hutt Curzon-Wylie to emerge, and when he did so Madar shot him dead. When another man, Doctor Lalcaca, tried to take the gun from Madar, he was also shot and killed. At his trial Madar said that the English were responsible for the deaths of millions of his countrymen and were an occupying force. He said he did not recognise the court but nevertheless thanked the judge when the verdict was passed, saying that he was proud to lay down his life for his country.

Richard Justin, age 31, convicted of the murder of step-daughter Annie Thompson. Executed at Belfast, 19 August 1909. Hangman: Henry Pierrepoint.

John Freeman, age 46, convicted of the murder of sister-in-law Florance Freeman. Executed at Hull, 7 December 1909. Hangman: Henry Pierrepoint.

Abel Atherton, age 29, convicted of the murder of Elizabeth Patrick. Executed at Durham, 8 December 1909. Hangman: Henry Pierrepoint.

Samuel Atherley, age 30, convicted of the murders of common-law wife, Matilda Lambert, and his children, John, Annie and Samuel. Executed at Nottingham, 14 December 1909. Hangman: Henry Pierrepoint.

1910

William Murphy, age 49, convicted of the murder of girlfriend Gwen Ellen Jones. Executed at Caernarfon, 15 February 1910. Hangman: Henry Pierrepoint.

Joseph Wren, age 23, convicted of the murder of John Collins. Executed at Manchester, 22 February 1910. Hangman: Henry Pierrepoint.

George Henry Perry, age 27, convicted of the murder of girlfriend Annie Covell. Executed at Pentonville, 1 March 1910. Hangman: Henry Pierrepoint.

Thomas Clements, age 62, convicted of the murders of Charles and Mary Thomas. Executed at Usk, 24 March 1910. Hangman: Henry Pierrepoint.

Thomas Jesshope, age 32, convicted of the murder of John Healy. Executed at Wandsworth, 25 May 1910. Hangman: Henry Pierrepoint.

James Henry Hancock, age 55, convicted of the murder of Alfred Dogget. Executed at Cambridge, 14 June 1910. Hangman: Henry Pierrepoint.

Thomas Craig, age 24, convicted of the murder of Thomas Henderson. Executed at Durham, 12 July 1910. Hangman: Henry Pierrepoint.

Frederick Foreman, age 45, convicted of the murder of girlfriend Elizabeth Ely. Executed at Chelmsford, 14 July 1910. Hangman: Henry Pierrepoint.

John Raper Coulson, age 32, convicted of the murder of wife and son, Jane and Thomas. Executed at Leeds, 9 August 1910. Hangman: Thomas Pierrepoint.

John Alexander Dickman, age 45, convicted of the murder of John Nisbet. Executed at Newcastle, 9 August 1910. Hangman: John Ellis.

John Rawcliffe, age 31, convicted of the murder of wife Louisa Ann. Executed at Lancaster, 15 November 1910. Hangman: John Ellis.

Henry Thompson, age 54, convicted of the murder of wife Mary. Executed at Liverpool, 22 November 1910. Hangman: John Ellis.

Hawley Harvin Crippen, 48, convicted of the murder of wife, Cora Turner. Executed at Pentonville, 23 November 1910. Hangman: John Ellis.

The Crippen case is one of the most infamous in the history of British murder. This is not because his crime was any different, any more terrible than the many other cases where husbands have killed their wives, but rather because his capture was noteworthy in that it was the first to involve the use of wireless telegraphy. Crippen and his mistress Ethel Le Neve were aboard the SS *Montrose*, taking the Atlantic crossing to Canada, when the ship's captain, Henry George Kendell, recognised Crippen as a fugitive, a man wanted in relation to a human torso found in the cellar of his London home. The captain immediately ordered his telegraphist to send the following message to the British authorities: 'Have strong suspicions that Crippen, London cellar murderer and accomplice are among saloon passengers. Moustache taken off, growing beard. Accomplice dressed as boy. Manner and build undoubtably a girl.'

Ethel, Crippen's lover, was disguised as a boy and travelling under the pretence of being Crippen's son, and the telegram prompted Chief Inspector Walter Dew to board the much faster SS *Laurentic* and arrive in Canada before Crippen. So, on 31 July 1910, Dew, together with two Canadian officers, boarded the *Montrose* as it sailed up the St. Lawrence, and arrested Crippen and Le Neve. Crippen would be tried for murder while Ethel would face charges of being an accessory to murder.

Crippen was convicted and hanged, while Le Neve was found not guilty and later married. She had two children and lived under the name of Ethel Smith until she died peacefully in 1967. Throughout his trial Crippen vehemently protested his innocence, claiming that his wife had run off to America with a man named Bruce Miller. The human torso found bricked up in the cellar must have been placed there by a previous inhabitant of the house at Hilltop Crescent, Holloway. The jury could not accept that a man, if he was innocent, would be travelling to Canada with his lover disguised as a boy.

The story has a postscript in that DNA evidence examined by American researchers in 2007 revealed that the remains found in Crippen's cellar were not in fact those of Cora Crippen, but were actually male. This raises questions as to the identity of the remains found in Crippen's cellar and, by extension, Crippen's guilt. In December 2009 the Criminal Cases Review Commission, having reviewed the case, announced that the Court of Appeal would not hear the case to pardon Crippen posthumously.

William Broome, age 26, convicted of the murder of Isabelle Wilson. Executed at Reading, 24 November 1910. Hangman: John Ellis.

Noah Woolf, age 58, convicted of the murder of Andrew Simon. Executed at Pentonville, 21 December 1910. Hangman: John Ellis.

Henry Ison, age 26, convicted of the murder of girlfriend Mary Jenkins. Executed at Leeds, 29 December 1910. Hangman: Thomas Pierrepoint.

Chapter Six

The Hangmen

It is said to be a deterrent, I can't agree. There have been murders since the beginning of time, and we shall continue to look for deterrents until the end of time. If death were a deterrent, I might be expected to know this. It is I who have faced them last, young lads and girls, workingmen, grandmothers. I have been amazed to see the courage with which they take that walk into the unknown. It did not deter them then, and it had not deterred them when they committed that which they had been convicted for. All the men and women whom I have faced at their final moment convince me that in what I have done I have not prevented a single murder...

Capital punishment, in my view, achieved nothing but revenge.

Albert Pierrepoint writing in his 1974 autobiography.

In the early days of capital punishment, hangmen were selected from men who lived in the manors and towns where the punishment was to take place. They would be paid by the civil authorities, and quite often the hangmen were criminals themselves who had been given a reprieve for taking up the distasteful duty of hangman. Their duties would also include administrating floggings, clearing the streets of swine, and various other duties handed out by the town council. There was no apprenticeship or training available, and if a county sheriff could not find a hangman he would have to carry out the task himself.

Perhaps the most famous executioner of all was Jack Ketch. Little is known of Ketch's early life, though it is believed that he hailed from Ireland and arrived in England as a young man. He was first appointed public hangman by King Charles II in 1663, and his notoriety stems largely from a number of botched executions over which he presided. In 1683 Ketch was said to have taken three blows to behead William Lord Russell for his part in the Rye House conspiracy, a plot to dispose Charles II. Ketch's first blow struck Russell in the shoulder and some contemporary reports claim he was being deliberately vindictive and trying to cause the nobleman as much pain as possible. There are statements written by witnesses which say that Ketch was blind drink as he wielded the axe.

Later, in 1865, Ketch botched the beheading of the Duke of Monmouth. This time Ketch took at least five blows with the axe, gave up halfway through and had to be ordered to finish the grisly task. He completed the job with a carving knife.

The great Victorian historian and statesman Lord Macaulay said of Ketch that he was a wretch who had butchered many a brave victim, and whose name has, during a century and a half, been given to many of those who succeeded him in his odious office.

Ketch died in 1687 leaving a legacy of killings so horrific that his name lives on in folklore and popular culture, even lending his name to the hangman in the Punch and Judy puppet show.

John Price was another famous hangman who was commonly (and rather confusingly) also known as Jack Ketch. He was appointed executioner in 1714 and held the position for four years before he himself was found guilty of murder and hanged. Price had served a prison term for failing to meet his debts and shortly after being released in 1718 he brutally raped and beat a young woman named Elizabeth White. Price was not the only hangman to face the rope himself, but he does hold the distinction of being the only one to also be gibbeted: his carcass hung on display in an iron cage in Holloway.

Records of those who held the office of Common Hangman were not always kept, and even when records were made it was often only the flimsiest of details that were recorded. For instance, we know that in 1538 London's official hangman, a man remembered only by the name Cartwell, was himself hanged for theft. Different regions had their own hangmen, and as previously noted these were often criminals themselves who had been granted a reprieve to carry out executions, and so a list of all those who have ever served as hangman is an impossibility. However, if we limit ourselves to London alone, we know that the following men served in office before the nineteenth century:

Thomas Derrick 1601–16
Gregory Brandon 1616–40
Richard Brandon 1640–49
William Lowen 1649
Edward Dunn 1649–63
Jack Ketch 1663–86

Paskah Rose 1686
John Price 1714–15
William Marvell 1715–17
Banks the Bailiff 1717–18
Richard Arnett 1726–8
John Hooper 1728–35
John Thrift 1735–52
Thormas Turlis 1752–71
Edward Dennis 1771–86
William Brunskill 1786–1814

Brunskill is notable in that among the incredible 537 people he hanged was John Bellingham, who had shot Prime Minister Spencer Percival, the only British Prime Minister ever to be assassinated.

Many of these hangmen were shunned, even hated by the public, but with William Calcraft, who held the office of London's hangman between 1829 and 1874, it was a different matter. Calcraft became the first celebrity hangman and very much a superstar of his day.

It is estimated that Calcraft hanged around 450 people, 35 of these being women. One of twelve children, he was born into a poor family, but he did particularly well in school and developed a head for business. As a young man he noticed the crowds that gathered at public hangings and realised they represented an opportunity. He began as a trader of snacks at executions, but his eyes were always watching the executioners and he soon made a move to enter that line of work himself. Initially he worked as a hangman's assistant at Lincoln, where he befriended a hangman named Foxton, and when Foxton was due to retire Calcraft put in an application for his job. 'You are a rum'un wanting to take up my line of business,' Foxton told Calcraft, 'for it is a despicable calling, a wretched occupation.'

Calcraft though was undeterred and wrote in his application, 'Gentlemen, having been informed that the office of hangman will soon be vacant, I beg very humbly to offer myself as a candidate. I am twenty-nine years of age, strong and robust, and have had some experience in the office. I am familiar with the mode of operation, having had some months ago, been engaged in an emergency to hang two men at Lincoln. I did so, and as the two culprits passed off without a struggle, the execution was performed to the entire satisfaction of the sheriff of the county.'

Calcraft had a competitor for the position, but this man had no experience as an executioner and so it was Calcraft who was the successful applicant, taking up his position in 1829, and during his first year in office he performed thirty-one executions. He favoured the short drop method of execution which meant the condemned was slowly strangled to death, but often he would help them on their way by pulling on their legs, or jumping on their backs swinging back and forth with them. His executions would attract crowds upwards of 30,000, he was regularly featured in newspaper reports, and he received both adoring letters and death threats. With the advent of the railway system, regional hangmen were no longer needed and Calcraft would travel across the land to carry out executions, and his fame spread throughout the country. He would employ young boys at his executions to mingle with the crowds and sell refreshments that he had provided. He would further supplement his income by selling the ropes and straps that had been used in his hangings.

Calcraft retired, somewhat reluctantly, in 1874, and received a pension of 25 shillings a week from the City of London. His final years were spent as a recluse, rarely venturing outside his home in Poole Street, where he died in his sleep in 1879.

William Marwood succeeded Calcraft as official hangman and he was to bring with him a very different attitude to the job. Public hangings had by this point been abolished and there was growing momentum for the reform and abolition of the death penalty, but politicians in favour of retaining the death penalty would point to Marwood's long drop system which was considered a humane way of despatching a culprit to the afterlife. Before taking over the role of official hangman, Marwood had worked as a regional hangman for his home town of Lincoln where he had developed his system in which the length of the drop was measured in relation to the height and weight of the condemned man or woman and this resulted in the neck being broken instantly.

Marwood was responsible for 176 hangings, many of high-profile criminals. Once such was that of Charles Peace whom Marwood hanged at Leeds in 1879. Peace was the most notorious villain in Britain until Jack the Ripper, and one of the most colourful. He had been born in 1832, the son of a shoemaker, and by the age of 12 he was working in a rolling mill in Sheffield called Millsands. It was here that an accident happened in which a red-hot bar impaled his left leg, leaving him with a limp and one finger less on his right hand. This all contributed to the grotesque figure he became in later life. While he was recovering from his accident, Peace took up the violin, becoming so adept at playing it that he was soon in demand at concerts, receiving good reviews for his performances.

Crime though supplemented Peace's earnings and he became a housebreaker, but in 1854 his luck ran out and he was apprehended by the police. He was found guilty of multiple burglaries and was sentenced to four years penal servitude. Following his release in 1859 he met and married a young widow named Hannah Ward. For a short period he seemed to be living a good life, but was soon back in the trouble with the law after being arrested for a major burglary in Manchester, for which he received six years penal servitude. When he eventually left prison, Peace seemed to be going straight and concentrated on a picture framing business he set up. But by 1876 he was up to his old tricks, and it was during another burglary in Manchester that he committed his first murder.

It was at Whalley Range, Manchester, that Peace was spotted by two policemen entering the grounds of a large house. One of the policemen, PC Nicholas Cock, intercepted Peace as he was making his exit, but Peace pulled a revolver and shot the policeman before making good his escape. Another man, William Habron, was tried and convicted of the policeman's murder, and Peace couldn't resist attending the trial, later saying that it was a grand spectacle.

Peace then returned to the Sheffield suburb of Darnall where he was now living, and became infatuated with one Mrs Katherine Dyson, the wife of his friend Arthur Dyson. The woman liked to drink and would often be seen about town with Peace until her husband grew jealous and threw a card stating: 'Peace is to stay away from my wife,' into the garden of Peace's home.

Later Peace saw Arthur and Katherine together and he threatened them, which resulted in Mr Dyson taking out a summons against Peace before moving to Banner Cross to put some distance between them. If the Dysons thought their moving home would be an end to the matter, they were wrong. On their first night in their new home, Katherine came outside to visit the outhouse when Peace suddenly appeared. She screamed, which brought her husband out of the house, and Peace turned and ran down an alleyway. Arthur Dyson went in pursuit, and Peace shot at him twice. The first shot went wide but the second hit the man squarely in the temple, killing him.

There was now a manhunt, with a sizeable reward for Peace. He changed his appearance somewhat, even disguising his missing finger with an ingenious prosthetic hand of his own creation. In 1877 Peace, together with his wife and son, set up home in a villa in Peckham. For a period, Peace lived under the name of John Ward and claimed to be a businessman and inventor. There was some truth in this since he invented and patented a device for raising sunken vessels and even attended the House of Commons to talk about his invention, but Peace simply couldn't stay away from criminal activities. An argument with his mistress, a Mrs Sue Thompson, led to her informing the police where Peace could be found.

Marwood hanged Peace on 25 February 1879, with the execution replacing the story of the the defence of Rorke's Drift on the front pages of the newspapers. The hangman was reported as telling the *Illustrated Police News*, 'He [Peace] was such a desperate man but bless you dear sir. He passed away like a summer's eve.'

This was not the only high profile hanging that Maywood was involved in and he began to receive death threats, but he ignored these and continued doing work across the country. At home in Lincoln he would often reside in an attic room of what is now the Castle Hill Club. He died in 1883 from pneumonia and jaundice and was buried in an unmarked grave at Trinity Church, Horncastle.

London's chief hangmen 1814-1910

John Langley 1814–17
James Booting 1817–20
James Foxen 1820–9
William Calcraft 1829–74
William Marwood 1874–83
Bartholomew Binns 1883–4
James Berry 1884–91
James Billington 1891–1901

Perhaps the best remembered hangmen, at least in modern times, were the Pierrepoints, who became known as the hanging family. The story began with Henry Pierrepoint who held the office of chief hangman in 1901-10. He worked with his brother Thomas as his assistant but was struck from the list of official executioners in 1910 after arriving drunk at Chelmsford for an execution. During the preparations for the execution he fought with his assistant John Ellis, and that was the end for Pierrepoint as the Britain's chief hangman. He would die in December 1922 at the age of 44 after a long illness.

In 1910, following Henry's removal from the role, it was his brother Thomas who became the chief hangman. During the period there were several approved hangmen on Home Office lists and Thomas would find himself working with different assistants. Indeed for a period before becoming chief hangman Thomas would find himself assistant to John Ellis, the man who had brought about his brother's downfall from the job. In the end Thomas would last for thirty-seven years in the office of hangman and was responsible for some 294 executions.

However, it was Henry's son Albert who would become the most famous hangman of the family, and was recently the subject of a critically acclaimed and commercially successful film with Timothy Spall in the leading role.

Albert would be responsible for more than 400 executions – some sources claim it was as many as 600. Among these were seventeen women, including Ruth Ellis, the last woman to be hanged in the UK.

Albert hanged the notorious traitor William (Lord Haw Haw) Joyce, as well as other high-profile killers such as John Haigh and John Christie. He was also responsible for hanging the Welshman Timothy Evans, who was convicted of killing his daughter but given a posthumous pardon in 1966 when it was discovered that John Christie was the real killer. This case, along with those of Derek Bentley and Ruth Ellis, both of whom were hanged by Albert Pierrepoint, played a major part in the abolition of capital punishment in the UK.

After the Second World War Albert Pierrepoint became a national hero when, at the behest of Field Marshall Montgomery, he was flown to Germany to preside over the hanging of many notable Nazis. During his first week in Germany he hanged forty-seven, and the official figures state that altogether Pierrepoint hanged 200 war criminals while in Germany.

Albert would resign his position in 1956 over a dispute about his wages, though there were stories in the press that claimed Pierrepoint had resigned because of doubts over the hanging of Ruth Ellis; but he denied this. After stepping down, Albert concentrated on his life as a publican, and in 1974 he published his autobiography, *Executioner Pierrepoint*. It was here that he revealed he no longer supported the death penalty and doubted that it was a deterrent. Albert Pierrepoint died in 1992 at the age of 87.

Home Office approved executioners, 1900 to abolition

Henry Pierrepoint 1900–10
John Ellis 1901–23
William Billington 1902–05
John Billington 1902–05
William Willis 1906–26
Thomas Pierrepoint 1906–46
Robert Baxter 1915–35
Thomas Phillips 1918–41

Robert Wilson 1920–36
Alfred Allen1928–37
Stanley Cross 1932–41
Albert Pierrepoint 1932–56
Henry Kirk 1941–50
Stephen Wade 1941–55
Herbert Henry Allen 1949–51
Robert Leslie Stuart 1950–64

Chapter Seven

Judicial Executions 1911-49

1911

George Newton, age 19, convicted of the murder of girlfriend Ada Roker. Executed at Chelmsford, 31 January 1911. Hangman: John Ellis.

Thomas Seymour, age 65, convicted of the murder of wife Mary. Executed at Liverpool, 6 May 1911. Hangman: John Ellis.

Michael Collins, age 26, convicted of the murder of girlfriend Elizabeth Kempster. Executed at Pentonville, 24 May 1911. Hangman: John Ellis.

Arthur Garrod, age 49, convicted of the murder of girlfriend Sarah Chilvers. Executed at Ipswich, 20 June 1911. Hangman: John Ellis.

William Henry Palmer, age 50, convicted of the murder of Ann Harris. Executed at Leicester, 19 July 1911. Hangman: John Ellis.

Francisco Charles Godhino, age 40, convicted of the murder of Alice Brewster. Executed at Pentonville, 17 October 1911. Hangman: John Ellis.

Edward Hill, age 41, convicted of the murder of wife Mary Jane. Executed at Pentonville, 17 October 1911. Hangman: John Ellis.

Fredrick Henry Thomas, age 38, convicted of the murder of girlfriend Harriet Ann Eckhart. Executed at Wandsworth, 15 November 1911. Hangman: John Ellis.

Michael Fagan, age 27, convicted of the murder of Lucy Kennedy. Executed at Liverpool, 6 December 1911. Hangman: John Ellis.

Walter Martin, age 22, convicted of the murder of girlfriend Edith Griffiths. Executed at Manchester, 12 December 1911. Hangman: John Ellis.

John Edward Tarkenter, age 41, convicted of the murder of wife Rosetta. Executed at Manchester, 12 December 1911. Hangman: John Ellis.

Henry Phillips, age 44, convicted of the murder of wife Margaret. Executed at Swansea, 14 December 1911. Hangman: John Ellis.

Joseph Fletcher, age 40, convicted of the murder of wife Caroline. Executed at Liverpool, 15 December 1911. Hangman: John Ellis.

George William Parker, age 26, convicted of the murder of girlfriend Mary Elizabeth Speller. Executed at Maidstone, 19 December 1911. Hangman: John Ellis.

Charles Coleman, age 36, convicted of the murder of Rose Ann Gurney. Executed at St Albans, 21 December 1911. Hangman: John Ellis.

George Loake, age 64, convicted of the murder of wife Elizabeth. Executed at Stafford, 28 December 1911. Hangman: Thomas Pierrepoint.

1912

Myer Abramovitch, age 28, convicted of the murders of Solomon and Annie Milstein. Executed at Pentonville, 6 March 1912. Hangman: John Ellis.
    A piece of trivia about this case: the murders occurred at 62 Hanbury Street, Spitalfields, virtually opposite the house where Jack the Ripper killed Annie Chapman.

John Williams, age 38, convicted of killing wife Hilda. Executed at Knutsford, 19 March 1912. Hangman: John Ellis.

Frederick Henry Seddon, age 40, convicted of the murder of Eliza Barrow. Executed at Pentonville, 18 April 1912. Hangman: John Ellis.
    A photograph taken in the courtroom while the death sentence was being passed is the only known photograph of a death sentence being passed in an English court. See photograph section.

Arthur Birkett, age 22, convicted of the murder of girlfriend Alice Beetham. Executed at Manchester, 23 July 1912. Hangman: John Ellis.

Sargent Phillip, age 33, convicted of the murder of wife Rose. Executed at Wandsworth, 1 October 1912. Hangman: John Ellis.

Robert Galloway, age 27, convicted of the murder of girlfriend Minni Morris. Executed at Norwich, 5 November 1912. Hangman: Thomas Pierrepoint.

Gilbert Oswald Smith, age 35, convicted of the murder of girlfriend Rosabella Smith. Executed at Gloucester, 26 November 1912. Hangman: Thomas Pierrepoint.

William Charles Beale, age 20, convicted of the murder of girlfriend Clara Elizabeth Carter. Executed at Chelmsford, 10 December 1912. Hangman: John Ellis.

Alfred John Lawrence, age 32, convicted of the murder of girlfriend Emily Violet Hubbard. Executed at Maidstone, 18 December 2018. Hangman: John Ellis.

William Wallace Galbraith, age 27, convicted of the murder of wife Mary May Galbraith. Executed at Wakefield, 20 December 1912. Hangman: Thomas Pierrepoint.

1913

Albert Rumens, age 44, convicted of the murder of Mabel Ann Maryan. Executed at Lewes, 7 January 1913. Hangman: John Ellis.
    Albert Rumens was the first person hanged at Lewes since 1892.

George MacKay, age 29, convicted of the murder of Arthur Wallis. Executed at Lewes, 29 January 1913. Hangman: John Ellis.

Edward Hopword, age 45, convicted of the murder of girlfriend Florence Alice Silles. Executed at Pentonville, 29 January 1913. Hangman: Thomas Pierrepoint.

Eric James Sedgewick, age 29, convicted of the murder of girlfriend Annie Davies. Executed at Reading, 4 February 1913. Hangman: John Ellis.

George Cunliffe, age 28, convicted of the murder of girlfriend Kate Butler. Executed at Exeter, 25 February 1913. Hangman: John Ellis.

Edward Henry Palmer, age 23, convicted of the murder of girlfriend Ada Louise James. Executed at Wakefield, 23 April 1913. Hangman: Thomas Pierrepoint.

Walter William Sykes, age 24, convicted of the murder of Amy Collinson and Francis Alice Nicholson. Executed at Wakefield, 23 April 1913. Hangman: Thomas Pierrepoint.

Sykes initially confessed to the murders and admitted to raping Amy, but later withdrew his confession, and the police were subsequently unable to provide any evidence to link him to the terrible crimes. However, due to the fact that he was unable to prove his whereabouts at the time of the murders the jury found him guilty.

William Walter Burton, age 29, convicted of the murder of girlfriend Winifred Mitchell. Executed at Dorchester, 24 June 1913. Hangman: Thomas Pierrepoint.

Henry Longden, age 52, convicted of the murder of girlfriend Alice Catlow Moore. Executed at Pentonville, 8 July 1913. Hangman: John Ellis.

Thomas Fletcher, age 28, convicted of the murder of girlfriend Lillian Wharton. Executed at Worcester, 9 July 1913. Hangman: John Ellis.

John Vickers Amos, age 35, convicted of the murders of Andrew Barton, George Bertram Mussel and Sarah Allen Grice. Executed at Newcastle, 22 July 1913. Hangman: Thomas Pierrepoint.

On the afternoon of 15 April 1913, the Sun Inn, a small public house in Bedlington, Northumberland, became the scene of a shootout that could have come from the Wild West. John Amos had been served an eviction notice from the Sun Inn where he worked as the landlord, but when the licensee, a Mr James Woodirons, turned up with the new tenants, Richard and Sarah Grice, along with policeman George Mussel, he pulled a Winchester from behind the bar. He shot Sarah Grice in the head and then shot George Mussel in the neck. When another policeman, Sergeant Andrew Barton, turned up and tried to talk to Amos, he too was shot dead. Amos then fled into the surrounding countryside where a miner took several shots at him, one striking him in the head but not killing him. He was then arrested and later faced the hangman.

Frank Greening, age 34, convicted of the murder of girlfriend Elizabeth Hearne. Executed at Birmingham, 13 August 1913. Hangman: Thomas Pierrepoint.

James Ryder, age 47, convicted of the murder of wife Ann. Executed at Manchester, 13 August 1913, Hangman: John Ellis.

Hugh McLaren, age 29, convicted of the murder of Julian Biros. Executed at Cardiff, 14 August 1913. Hangman: John Ellis.

Patrick Higgins, age 38, convicted of the murders of sons William and John Higgins. Executed at Edinburgh, 2 October 1913. Hangman: John Ellis.

On June 5 1913, Thomas Duncan made a grisly discovery in the waters of Hopetown Quarry, West Lothian. Floating among the weeds were the remains of two young boys who had been tied together and thrown into the water. It would be established that the boys were 6-year-old William Higgins and his 4-year-old brother Tom and that they had been in the water since late 1911. The boy's father, widower Patrick Higgins was arrested and later charged with the murders. Investigations would reveal that Higgins had killed them to save himself the cost of their upkeep.

Frederick Seekings, age 39, convicted of the murder of girlfriend Martha Beeby. Executed at Cambridge, 4 November 1913. Hangman: Thomas Pierrepoint.

Augustus John Penny, age 30, convicted of the murder of mother Matilda. Executed at Winchester, 26 November 1913. Hangman: John Ellis.

Frederick Albert Robinson, age 26, convicted of the murder of his children, Nellie, Fredrick and Beatrice. Executed at Pentonville, 27 November 1913. Hangman: John Ellis.

Ernest Edward Kelly, age 20, convicted of the murder of Daniel Bardsley. Executed at Manchester, 17 December 1913. Hangman: John Ellis.

George Fredrick Law, age 34, convicted of the murder of Annie Cotterill. Executed at Wakefield, 31 December 1913. Hangman: Thomas Pierrepoint.

1914

George Ball, age 22, convicted of the murder of Christina Bradfield. Executed at Liverpool, 26 February 1914. Hangman: John Ellis.

Josiah Davies, age 58, convicted of the murder of Martha Hodges. Executed at Stafford, 10 March 1914. Hangman: John Ellis.

James Honeyands, age 21, convicted of the murder of Amelia Bradfield. Executed at Exeter, 12 March 1914. Hangman: John Ellis.

Robert Upton, age 50, convicted of the murder of Charles Gribbin. Executed at Durham, 24 March 1914. Hangman: John Ellis.

Edgar Lewis George Bindon, age 19, convicted of the murder of girlfriend Maud Mulholland. Executed at Cardiff, 25 March 1914. Hangman: John Ellis.

Joseph Spooner, age 41, convicted of the murder of daughter Elizabeth. Executed at Liverpool, 14 March 1914. Hangman: William Willis.

Walter James White, age 22, convicted of the murder of girlfriend Francis Hunter. Executed at Winchester, 16 June 1914. Hangman: John Ellis.

Herbert Brooker, age 32, convicted of the murder of girlfriend Ada Stone. Executed at Lewes, 28 July 1914. Hangman: John Ellis.

Percy Edward Clifford, age 32, convicted of the murder of wife Maud. Executed at Lewes, 11 August 1914. Hangman: John Ellis.

Charles Frembd, age 71, convicted of the murder of Louisa Frembd. Executed at Chelmsford, 4 November 1914. Hangman: John Ellis.

Carl Hans Lody, age not recorded in legal records, convicted of spying. Executed at the Tower of London, 6 November 1914. Shot by firing squad.
    As soon as hostilities broke out between Britain and Germany, Carl Lody, a patriotic officer in the German Naval Reserve, offered his service to his country. He was sent to Britain with a stolen American passport. He was arrested in Ireland while spying on the naval base at Queenstown. Lody was the first man shot at the Tower during the First World War.

John Frances Eayres, age 59, convicted of the murder of wife Sarah. Executed at Northampton, 10 November 1914.

Henry Quartley, age 55, convicted of the murder of Henry Pugsley. Executed at Shepton Mallet, 10 November 1914. Hangman: Thomas Pierrepoint.

Arnold Warren, age 32, convicted of the murder of son James. Executed at Leicester, 12 November 1914. Hangman: John Ellis.

George Anderson, age 59, convicted of the murder of stepdaughter Harriet Ann Whybrow. Executed at St Albans, 23 December 1914. Hangman: John Ellis.

1915

Carl Frederick Muller, age 58, convicted of spying. Executed by firing squad at the Tower of London, 23 June 1915.

Robert Rosenthal, age 22, convicted of spying. Executed by firing squad at the Tower of London, 15 July 1915.

Haicke Marinus Janssen and Willem Johannes Roos, aged 29 and 33, convicted of spying. Executed by firing squad at the Tower of London, 30 July 1915.

Walter Marriott, age 24, convicted of the murder of wife Nellie. Executed at Wakefield, 10 August 1915. Hangman: Thomas Pierrepoint.

Frank Steele, age 28, convicted of the murder of girlfriend Nora Barrett. Executed at Durham, 11 August 1915. Hangman: John Ellis.

George Joseph Smith, age 43, convicted of the murders of wives (bigamous), Beatrice Constance Mundy, Alice Burnham and Margaret Elizabeth Lofty. Executed at Maidstone, 13 August 1913. Hangman: John Ellis.

Known to history as the Brides in the Bath Killer, George Joseph Smith was a striking looking man with 'the gift of the gab', and wherever he went he left a string of broken hearts behind him. He was born in Bethnal Green in 1872 and by the time he was 10 years old he found himself in a reform school following a catalogue of petty thefts. He left the school at 16 and soon found himself serving a six-month prison term for stealing a bicycle. He was released in 1891 and then served three years in the army.

No sooner was he out of the army than he found himself back in prison, this time serving his sentence under the false name of George Baker. He had been handed a twelve-month term for larceny and receiving, but had the courts been aware of his real identity, and string of convictions, then it is likely he would have received a considerably longer sentence.

Upon release, Smith moved to Leicester and opened a barbershop at Russell Square. By this point he was using the name Oliver Love, and soon he met a young woman named Caroline Thornhill. After a whirlwind romance they were married on 17 January 1898, but the bride's family were horrified and boycotted the wedding ceremony. They kept pressure on Caroline and this resulted in her leaving her new husband and going to live with a cousin in Nottingham. But Smith, still posing as Oliver Love, followed her and persuaded her to come back to him. The young couple then moved to London, then Brighton, then Hove and finally Hastings. Here Caroline, using false references written by Smith, found work as a domestic servant. She would, at Smith's bidding, steal from the homes of her employers until she was caught and arrested in 1899. She received a six-month prison sentence while Smith ran off to London and married his landlady.

Caroline was released from prison in 1900 and when visiting London one afternoon she saw a face from the past. Across the road from her was the man she knew as Oliver Love, the man who had been responsible for her being sent to prison. She quickly found a policeman and reported her husband, which resulted in Smith, still using the name Oliver Love, finding himself in court. On 9 January 1901 he was given a two-year sentence for receiving stolen goods.

October 1903 saw Smith a free man and he became a dealer in second-hand goods. He would travel the country, preying on gullible women as he went. In 1908 he was back in Brighton where he met and married widow Florence Wilson, whom he swindled of her savings and disappeared from her life forever.

In July of that year he was in Bristol where he married another woman, Edith Peglar, who joined him on his travels across the country. By 1909 he had grown bored of Edith and he married yet another woman, Sarah Freeman. After relieving her of £300 in savings, he abandoned her at London's National Gallery.

By now Smith had amassed a considerable sum of money and he started investing in property. In Southend he bought 22 Glenmore Street and then in Bristol he bought 86 Ashley Down Road. As a wealthy man he found it even easier to meet young women who he would persuade to part with their savings. But in 1910 he took the first step that would turn him into a killer. Smith was in Clifton when he met Bessie Mundy and soon learned that she had more than £2,000 – a fortune – in her bank account. Using the name Henry Williams, he romanced Bessie and they were married at Weymouth on 26 August 1910. However Smith soon learned that Bessie's money was held in a trust and she couldn't get at it, so Smith left her, writing a letter implying that she had given him venereal disease.

Smith went back to Bristol, and in 1912 found himself in Weston-super-Mare where he once again bumped into Bessie. He set about romancing her until she took him back and together they moved into a rented house at Herne Bay.

Smith now had murder on his mind. He knew that he could not get his hands on the money Bessie had in trust, but if she died leaving a favourable will then he would inherit the money. So he and Bessie each made wills in favour of each other.

On 9 July Smith bought a new tin bath and had it delivered to the home he shared with Bessie. A day later he took Bessie to a doctor, telling him that she had had a fit, but the doctor could find nothing wrong with the women. The doctor prescribed a mild sedative and then two days later was called to visit Bessie at home. Again the doctor could find nothing wrong with the woman but her husband seemed deeply concerned. When he visited on 13 July, Bessie was dead. The doctor found Bessie naked in the bathtub, her head beneath the water, and she couldn't be revived. Death by misadventure was recorded. Smith returned the bathtub to the ironmongers, getting his money back from the sympathetic storekeeper, and then sold off most of the furniture from the house he had shared with Bessie.

Bessie's relatives were suspicious and tried to contest the will, but they were unsuccessful, and Smith received £2,500. He then went back to Bristol, bought several more houses and opened a string of bank accounts in different names. It had all worked out well for him, and Smith decided that this was the way forward.

In October 1913, Smith was in Southsea where he met Alice Burnham and, as was usual, he swept her off her feet and they were married. Smith insured his new wife's life for £500 and on 10 December the couple went to Blackpool and checked into a guesthouse. Smith then took his new wife to see a doctor. They complained that Alice had a fierce headache and the doctor prescribed some painkillers and a powder to clear her bowels.

On the evening of 12 December Smith asked the landlady's daughter to run a bath for his wife who, he told the young girl, was not feeling very well. And then at about quarter past eight that evening, Smith came into the kitchen and gave his landlady two eggs, asking if she would prepare them for breakfast in the morning. It was at that point that the landlady observed water coming through the ceiling. Smith ran up the stairs and then returned a moment later shouting, 'Fetch a doctor. My wife can't speak to me.'

All attempts to revive Alice failed and the doctor concluded that she must have drowned in her own bath. She was buried on 15 December and Smith collected on her insurance.

In September 1914 Smith, using the name Charles Oliver James, met and married Alice Reavil at Woolwich in London. The woman was a poor domestic servant but she was poorer still in by the end of that month when Smith ran off with her savings of £78.

Smith then married Margaret Lofty in December of the same year. The wedding took place in Bath and Smith, knowing that his new wife was insured for £700, set about planning her demise. They moved into rooms in Highgate, London, and soon the usual scenario was enacted. Smith took his wife to see a doctor, saying that she was having violent headaches. Shortly afterwards Margaret made a will leaving everything to her new husband. On 18 December Smith ran to see his landlady, telling her he had found his wife dead in the bath. Margaret was buried on 21 December and because she had been married for just two days, the story was considered especially tragic and it made front-page news. The story was seen by both Joseph Croxley, the landlord of the guesthouse in Blackpool, and Alice Burnham's father. Both went to the police.

On 4 January 1915 Smith visited his solicitor on Uxbridge Road only to find the police waiting for him. He was charged with bigamy and arrested. But the police were only holding him on the charge while they built the much more serious case of multiple murder. The bodies of Smith's three wives were exhumed, and then on 23 March he was charged with all three murders.

George Marshall, age 45, convicted of the murder of girlfriend Alice Anderson. Executed at Wandsworth, 17 August 1915. Hangman: John Ellis.

Ernest Waldemar Melin and Augusto Roggen, aged 49 and 34, jointly convicted of spying. Executed by firing squad at the Tower of London, 10 and 17 September 1915.

Fernando Buschman, age 25, convicted of spying. Executed by firing squad at the Tower of London, 19 October 1915.

George T. Breeckow, age 33, convicted of spying. Executed by firing squad at the Tower of London, 25 October 1915.

Iving Guy Ries, age 50, convicted of spying. Executed by firing squad at the Tower of London, 27 October 1915.

William Benjamin Reeve, age 42, convicted of the murder of wife Harriet. Executed at Bedford, 16 November 1915. Hangman: John Ellis.

Albert Meyer, age 23, convicted of spying. Executed by firing squad at the Tower of London, 27 November 1915.

John James Thornley, age 26, convicted of the murder of girlfriend Frances Johnson. Executed at Liverpool, 1 December 1915. Hangman: John Ellis.

Young Hill, age 28, convicted of the murder of James Crawford. Executed at Liverpool, 1 December 1915. Hangman: John Ellis.

Harry Thompson, age 55, convicted of the murder of girlfriend Alice Kaye. Executed at Wakefield, 22 December 1915. Hangman: Thomas Pierrepoint.

John William McCartney, age 40, convicted of the murder of bigamous wife, Charlotte McCartney. Executed at Wakefield, 29 December 1915. Hangman: Thomas Pierrepoint.

1916

Leo Kun, age 27, convicted of the murder of girlfriend Clara Thomas. Executed at Pentonville, 1 January 1916. Hangman: John Ellis.

Frederick Holmes, age 44, convicted of the murder of girlfriend Sarah Woodall. Executed at Manchester, 8 March 1916. Hangman: John Ellis.

Reginald Heath, age 25, convicted of the murder of Isabella Holmes Conway. Executed at Manchester, 29 March 1916. Hangman: John Ellis.

Ludovico Hurwitz y Zender, age 37, convicted of spying. Executed by firing squad at the Tower of London, 11 April 1916.

Roger David Casement, age 52, convicted of treason. Executed at Pentonville, 3 August 1916. Hangman: John Ellis.

William Alan Butler, age 39, convicted of the murder of Florence Beatrice Butler. Executed at Birmingham, 16 August 1916. Hangman: John Ellis.

Daniel Sullivan, age 38, convicted of the murder of wife Catherine. Executed at Swansea, 6 September 1916. Hangman: John Ellis.

Frederick Brooks, age 28, convicted of the murder of Alice Clara Gregory. Executed at Exeter, 12 December 1916. Hangman: John Ellis.

James Howarth Hargreaves, age 54, convicted of the murder of girlfriend Caroline McGhee. Executed at Manchester, 19 December 1916. Hangman: John Ellis.

Joseph Deans, age 44, convicted of the murder of girlfriend Catherine Convery. Executed at Durham, 20 December 1916. Hangman: John Ellis.

1917

Thomas Clinton, age 28, convicted of the murder of Henry Lynch. Executed at Manchester, 21 March 1917. Hangman: John Ellis.

John William Thompson, age 43, convicted of the murder of Lily Tindale. Executed at Leeds, 27 March 1917. Hangman: Thomas Pierrepoint.

Leo George O'Donnell, age 26, convicted of the murder of William F. Watterton. Executed at Winchester, 29 March 1917. Hangman: John Ellis.

Alec Bakerlis, age 24, convicted of the murder of girlfriend Winifred Ellen Fortt. Executed at Cardiff, 10 April 1917. Hangman: John Ellis.

William James Robinson, age 26, convicted of the murder of Alfred Williams. Executed at Pentonville, 17 April 1917. Hangman: John Ellis.

Robert Gadsby, age 65, convicted of the murder of girlfriend Julia Ann Johnson. Executed at Leeds, 18 April 1917. Hangman: Thomas Pierrepoint.

Thomas McGuiness, age 25, convicted of the murder of Alexander Imlach. Executed at Glasgow, 16 May 1917. Hangman: John Ellis.

William Thomas Hodgson, age 34, convicted of the murders of wife Margaret Alderson Hodgson and infant daughter Margaret. Executed at Liverpool, 16 August 1917. Hangman: John Ellis.

William Cavanagh, age 29, convicted of the murder of Henry Hollyer. Executed at Newcastle, 18 December 1917. Hangman: Thomas Pierrepoint.

Thomas Cox, age 59, convicted of the murder of wife, Elizabeth Cox. Executed at Shrewsbury, 19 December 1917. Hangman: John Ellis.

1918

Arthur de Stamir, age 26, convicted of the murder of Edward Tighe. Executed at Wandsworth, 12 February 1918. Hangman: John Ellis.

Joseph Jones, age 26, convicted of the murder of Oliver Gilbert. Executed at Wandsworth, 21 February 1918. Hangman: John Ellis.

Louis Voisin, age 50, convicted of the murder of Émilienne Gérard. Executed at Pentonville, 2 March 1918. Hangman: John Ellis.

Verney Hasser, age 30, convicted of the murder of Joseph Durkin. Executed at Shepton Mallet, 5 March 1918. Hangman: John Ellis.

Louis Van Kerkhove, age 32, convicted of the murder of girlfriend Clemence Verelst. Executed at Birmingham, 9 April 1918. Hangman: John Ellis.

John William Walsh, age 35, convicted of the murder of girlfriend Ruth Moore. Executed at Leeds, 17 December 1918. Hangman: Thomas Pierrepoint.

William Rooney, age 51, convicted of the murder of sister-in-law Mary Rooney. Executed at Manchester, 17 December 1918. Hangman: John Ellis.

1919

Benjamin Hindle Benson, age 41, convicted of the murder of girlfriend Annie Mayne. Executed at Leeds, 7 January 1919. Hangman: Thomas Pierrepoint.

George Walter Cardwell and Percy Barrett, aged 22 and 20, jointly convicted of the murder of Rhoda Walker. Executed at Leeds, 8 January 1918. Hangman: Thomas Pierrepoint.

Joseph Rose, age 25, convicted of the murder of girlfriend Sarah Rose and infant daughter Isabella. Executed at Oxford, 19 February 1919. Hangman: John Ellis.

Henry Beckett, age 36, convicted of the murders of Walter Cornish, Alice Cornish, Alice Cornish (daughter of Alice Cornish senior) and Marie Cornish. Executed at Pentonville, 10 July 1918. Hangman: John Ellis.

Henry Beckett was a soldier in the Army Veterinary Corps and finding himself due to be demobbed he was grateful to find lodgings in the home of the Cornish family at Stukeley Road, London. The lodgings seemed ideal, but five weeks after moving in Beckett found himself ordered to leave after arguing with Alice. This would spark off four brutal murders.

On the afternoon of 28 April 1919 Beckett returned to the Cornish house and finding only Alice at home he went inside and struck her with a poker from the fireplace. The blow didn't kill her and Beckett carried her to the garden shed and hit her with an axe and then stabbed her in the throat.

The next person to come home was 6-year-old Marie. Beckett struck her across the back of the head with a hammer and tossed her body down the cellar. Then 15-year-old Marie returned home and Beckett used the same hammer on her that he had used on her sister. She was also tossed down the cellar stairs. Walter Cornish arrived home and Beckett attacked him with the hammer, but there was a struggle in which Beckett struck the man several times with the axe and then fled. Walter died two days later in hospital but not before telling the police who they were looking for.

John Crossland, age 34, convicted of the murder of wife Ellen. Executed at Liverpool, 22 July 1919. Hangman: John Ellis.

Thomas Foster, age 46, convicted of the murder of wife Minnie. Executed at Pentonville, 31 July 1919. Hangman: John Ellis.

Henry Thomas Gaskin, age 27, convicted of the murder of wife Elizabeth. Executed at Birmingham, 8 August 1919. Hangman: John Ellis.

Frank George Warren, age 41, convicted of the murder of Lucy Nightingale. Executed at Pentonville, 7 October 1919. Hangman: John Ellis.

James Adams, age 32, convicted of the murder of girlfriend Mary Doyle. Executed at Glasgow, 11 November 1919. Hangman: John Ellis.

Ernest Scott, age 28, convicted of the murder of girlfriend Rebecca Quinn. Executed at Newcastle, 26 November 1919. Hangman: John Ellis.

Ambrose Quinn, age 28, convicted of the murder of wife Elizabeth. Executed at Newcastle, 26 November 1919. Hangman: John Ellis.
   By coincidence Ambrose Quinn followed Ernest Scott to the gallows. Scott had been convicted of murdering his girlfriend Rebecca Quinn, but other than surname there was no relation between the two.

Djang Djing Sung, age 33, convicted of the murder of Zee Ming Wu. Executed at Worcester, 3 December 1919. Hangman: John Ellis.

1920

Lewis Massey, age 29, convicted of the murder of wife Margaret Hird Massey. Executed at Leeds, 6 January 1920. Hangman: Thomas Pierrepoint.

Hyman Perdovitch, age 39, convicted of the murder of Soloman Franks. Executed at Manchester, 15 August 1920. Hangman: John Ellis.

David Caplan, age 42, convicted of the murder of wife Freda and sons Herman and Maurice. Executed at Manchester, 6 January 1918. Hangman: John Ellis.

William Wright, age 39, convicted of the murder of girlfriend Annie Coulbrook. Executed at Lincoln, 10 March 1920. Hangman: Thomas Pierrepoint.

William Hall, age 66, convicted of the murder of girlfriend Mary Ann Dixon. Executed at Durham, 23 March 1920. Hangman: John Ellis.

Frederick Rothwell Holt, age 32, convicted of the murder of girlfriend Kathleen Breaks. Executed at Manchester, 13 April 1920. Hangman: John Ellis.

Thomas Caler, age 23, convicted of the murders of Gladys May Ibrahim and infant Aysha Ibrahim. Executed at Cardiff, 14 April 1920. Hangman: John Ellis.

Miles McHugh, age 32, convicted of the murder of girlfriend Edith Annie Swainston. Executed at Leeds, 16 April 1920. Hangman: Thomas Pierrepoint.

Thomas Wilson, age 45, convicted of the murder of wife Annie Maria Wilson. Executed at Leeds, 6 May 1920. Hangman: Thomas Pierrepoint.

Herbert Sailsbury, age 35, convicted of the murder of girlfriend Alice Pearson. Executed at Liverpool, 11 May 1920. Hangman: John Ellis.

William Waddington, age 35, convicted of the murder of Ivy Wolfenden. Executed at Liverpool, 11 May 1920. Hangman: John Ellis.

Albert James Frazer and James Rollings, aged 24 and 22, jointly convicted of the murder of Henry Senior. Executed at Glasgow, 26 May 1920. Hangman: John Ellis.

Frederick William Storey, age 45, convicted of the murder of girlfriend Sarah Jane Howard. Executed at Ipswich, 16 June 1920. Hangman: John Ellis.

William Thomas Aldred, age 54, convicted of the murder of Ida Prescott. Executed at Manchester, 22 June 1920. Hangman: John Ellis.

Arthur Andrew Clement Goslett, age 44, convicted of the murder of wife Evelyn. Executed at Pentonville, 27 July 1920. Hangman: John Ellis.

James Ellor, age 35, convicted of the murder of wife Ada. Executed at Liverpool, 11 August 1920. Hangman: John Ellis.

James Riley, age 50, convicted of the murder of wife Mary. Executed at Durham, 30 November 1920. Hangman: Thomas Pierrepoint.

Cyril Victor Tennyson Saunders, age 21, convicted of the murder of girlfriend Dorthy May Saunders. Executed at Exeter, 30 November 1920. Hangman: John Ellis.

Marks Goodmacher, age 47, convicted of the murder of daughter, Fanny Zetoun. Executed at Pentonville, 30 December 1920. Hangman: William Willis.

Edwin Sowerby, age 28, convicted of the murder of girlfriend Jane Darwell. Executed at Leeds, 30 December 1920. Hangman: Thomas Pierrepoint.

Samuel Westwood, age 26, convicted of the murder of wife Lydia. Executed at Birmingham, 30 December 1920. Hangman: John Ellis.

Charles Colclough, age 45, convicted of the murder of George Henry Shenton. Executed at Manchester, 31 December 1920. Hangman: John Ellis.

1921

George Edwin Quinton Lever, age 51, convicted of the murder of wife Harriet. Executed at Maidstone, 7 January 1921. Hangman: Thomas Pierrepoint.

Jack Alfred Field and William Thomas, aged 19 and 29, jointly convicted of the murder of Irene Violet Munro. Executed at Wandsworth, 4 February 1920. Hangman: Thomas Pierrepoint.

George Bailey, age 22, convicted of the murder of wife Kate. Executed at Oxford, 2 March 1921. Hangman: John Ellis.

Frederick Quarmby, age 47, convicted of the murder of girlfriend Christine Smith. Executed at Manchester, 6 May 1921. Hangman: John Ellis.

Thomas Wilson, age 43, convicted of the murder of Olive Jackson. Executed at Manchester, 24 May 1921. Hangman: John Ellis.

Lester Augustus Hamilton, age 25, convicted of the murder of girlfriend Doris Appleton. Executed at Cardiff, 16 August 1921. Hangman: John Ellis.

Edward O'Connor, age 43, convicted of the murder of son Thomas. Executed at Birmingham, 22 December 1921. Hangman: John Ellis.

1922

William Harkness, age 31, convicted of the murder of Elizabeth Benjamin. Executed at Glasgow, 21 February 1922. Hangman: John Ellis.

James Hutton Williamson, age 37, convicted of the murder of wife Mary. Executed at Durham, 21 March 1922. Hangman: Thomas Pierrepoint.

William Sullivan, age 41, convicted of the murder of Margaret Thomas. Executed at Usk, 23 March 1922. Hangman: John Ellis.

Edward Ernest Black, age 36, convicted of the murder of wife Annie. Executed at Exeter, 24 March 1922. Hangman: John Ellis.

Percy James Atkin, age 29, convicted of the murder of wife Maud. Executed at Nottingham, 7 April 1922. Hangman: John Ellis.

Frederick Alexander Keeling, age 54, convicted of the murder of Emily Dewberry. Executed at Pentonville, 11 April 1922. Hangman: John Ellis.

Edmund Hugh Tonbridge, age 38, convicted of the murder of girlfriend Margaret Evans. Executed at Pentonville, 18 April 1922. Hangman: John Ellis.

Hiram Thompson, age 52, convicted of the murder of wife Ellen. Executed at Manchester, 30 May 1922. Hangman: John Ellis.

Herbert Rowes Armstrong, age 53, convicted of the murder of wife Katherine. Executed at Gloucester, 31 May 1922. Hangman: John Ellis.

Henry Julius Jacoby, age 18, convicted of the murder of Alice White. Executed at Pentonville, 7 June 1922. Hangman: John Ellis.

Joseph O' Sullivan and Reginald Dunne, aged 25 and 24, jointly convicted of the murder of Field Marshal Sir Henry Wilson. Executed at Wandsworth, 10 August 1922. Hangman: John Ellis.
     'You may kill my body, my lord, but my spirit you will never kill,' Joseph O'Sullivan told the judge as the death sentence was handed down to him and his accomplice Reginald Dunne. Both men were Irish Republicans and together on 22 June 1922 they had knocked on the door of the field marshal and opened fire.

Elijah Pountney, age 48, convicted of the murder of wife Alice. Executed at Birmingham, 11 August 1922. Hangman: John Ellis.

Simon McGeowen, age 38, convicted of the murder of Maggie Fullerton. Executed at Belfast, 17 August 1922. Hangman: John Ellis.

Thomas Henry Allaway, age 36, convicted of the murder of Irene May Wilkins. Executed at Winchester, 19 August 1922. Hangman: John Ellis.

William James Yeldham, age 23, convicted of the murder of George Grimshaw. Executed at Pentonville, 5 September 1922. Hangman: John Ellis.

George Robinson, age 27, convicted of the murder of girlfriend Frances Pacey. Executed at Lincoln, 13 December 1922. Hangman: Thomas Pierrepoint.

Frank Fowler, age 35, convicted of the murder of Ivy Prentice. Executed at Lincoln, 13 December 1922. Hangman: Thomas Pierrepoint.

William Rider, 40, convicted of the murder of wife Rosilla. Executed at Birmingham, 19 December 1922. Hangman: John Ellis.

1923

George Fredrick Edisbury, age 44, convicted of the murder of Winifred Drinkwater. Executed at Manchester, 3 January 1923. Hangman: John Ellis.

Lee Doon, 27, convicted of the murder of Sing Lee. Executed at Leeds, 5 January 1923. Hangman: Thomas Pierrepoint.

Edith Thompson and Frederick Bywaters, aged 30 and 21, jointly convicted of the murder of Percy Thompson. Executed at Holloway, 9 January 1923. Hangman: Thomas Pierrepoint.

William Rooney, age 40, convicted of the murder of Lily Johnston. Executed at Londonderry, 8 February 1923. Hangman: William Willis.

George Perry, age 50, convicted of the murder of sister-in-law Emma Perry. Executed at Manchester, 28 March 1923. Hangman: John Ellis.

Daniel Cassidy, age 60, convicted of the murder of Bernard Quinn. Executed at Durham, 3 April 1923. Hangman: Thomas Pierrepoint.

Bernard Pomroy, age 25, convicted of the murder of girlfriend Alice Cheshire. Executed at Pentonville, 5 April 1923. Hangman: John Ellis.

Frederick Wood, age 29, convicted of the murder of Margaret White. Executed at Liverpool, 10 April 1923. Hangman: John Ellis.

John Henry Savage, age 50, convicted of the murder of Wilhelmina Nicolson. Executed at Edinburgh, 11 June 1923. Hangman: John Ellis.

Rowland Duck, age 25, convicted of the murder of Nellie Pearce. Executed at Pentonville, 4 July 1923. Hangman: John Ellis.

William Griffiths, age 57, convicted of the murder of mother Catherine Hughes. Executed at Shrewsbury, 24 July 1923. Hangman: John Ellis.

Albert Edward Burrows, age 62, convicted of the murders of wife (bigamous) Hannah Calladine, son Albert Edward Calladine, Elsie Calladine, and Thomas Wood. Executed at Nottingham, 8 August 1923. Hangman: John Ellis.

Albert Burrows had made a mess of his life and in 1918 had been imprisoned for bigamy after marrying Hannah Calladine while already married. The pair had had a son, Albert Edward, and when Burrows was released from prison he went to live with Hannah since his legal wife no longer wanted anything to do with him. Burrows found himself having to pay maintenance to his legal wife and was soon in financial difficulties. His answer to this was to murder Hannah, his young son and Hannah's daughter from her first marriage and then dump their bodies down a disused mineshaft situated at a desolate spot on Simmondley Moor, Glossop.

Burrows then returned to his legal wife, telling her that Hannah and the children had gone away to live with family, he was not sure where. For the next three years Burrows seemingly lived the life of a devoted husband, but that was to change in 1923 when a 4-year-old child, Thomas Wood, went missing from home. Burrows had been seen talking to the boy shortly before his disappearance and when police questioned him, he broke down and took them to the disused mineshaft where he had dumped the body. The boy had been murdered and sexually abused and Burrows was arrested and charged with the dreadful crime. It was eight weeks later that police found the skeletons of Hannah Calladine and her two children in the disused mine.

Hassen Mohamed, age 33, convicted of the murder of girlfriend Jane Nagi. Executed at Durham, 8 August 1923. Hangman: Thomas Pierrepoint.

Susan Newell, age 30, convicted of the murder of John Johnston. Executed at Glasgow, 10 October 1923. Hangman: John Ellis.

Phillip Murray, age 31, convicted of the murder of William Cree. Executed at Edinburgh, 30 October 1923. Hangman: John Ellis.

Frederick William Jessie, age 26, convicted of the murder of aunt Mabel Edmunds. Executed at Wandsworth, 1 November 1923. Hangman: John Ellis.

John William Eastwood, age 39, convicted of the murder of John Clarke. Executed at Leeds, 28 December 1923. Hangman: John Ellis.

1924

Mathew Frederick Nunn, age 24, convicted of the murder of girlfriend Minetta Mary Kelly. Executed at Durham, 2 January 1924. Hangman: Thomas Pierrepoint.

Nunn's execution went terribly wrong, though at the time the authorities denied there had been any problems. It was later revealed that when Pierrepoint opened the trapdoor, the rope snapped and Nunn, half strangled, fell into the pit. The condemned man had to be returned to his cell and wait a further hour until the apparatus was ready for him to be hanged a second time. Thomas Pierrepoint was suspended from his duties while an official inquiry was held, but he was cleared of any wrongdoing and was back as chief hangman by June of that year.

Francis Wilson Brooker, age 28, convicted of the murder of Percy Sharp. Executed at Manchester, 8 April 1924. Hangman: William Willis.

Michael Pratley, age 30, convicted of the murder of Nelson Leech. Executed at Belfast, 8 May 1924. Hangman: William Willis.

William Horsely Wardell, age 47, convicted of the murder of Elizabeth Reaney. Executed at Leeds, 18 June 1924. Hangman: Thomas Pierrepoint.

Abraham Goldenberg, age 22, convicted of the murder of William Edward Hall. Executed at Winchester, 30 July 1924. Hangman: Thomas Pierrepoint.

Jean Pierre Vacquier, age 45, convicted of the murder of Alfred George Jones. Executed at Wandsworth, 12 August 1924. Hangman: Thomas Pierrepoint.

John Charles Horner, age 23, convicted of the murder of Norman Widdowsen Pinchin. Executed at Manchester, 13 August 1924. Hangman: William Willis.

   The body of 5-year-old Norman Pinchin was found at the bottom of a canal in Salford and the official cause of death was shock, but the shock had been brought on by the fact that he had been brutally raped and then thrown like rubbish into the canal. John Charles Horner had been seen walking off with the boy on the afternoon of 10 June 1924 and another witness, a man named Harry Barnes, saw Horner throwing the boy into the canal, which was why the police dredged the canal and found the child's body.

Patrick Herbert Mahon, age 34, convicted of the murder of girlfriend Emily Kays. Executed at Wandsworth, 3 September 1924, Hangman: Thomas Pierrepoint.

Frederick Southgate, age 52, convicted of the murder of wife Elizabeth. Executed at Ipswich, 27 November 1924. Hangman: Thomas Pierrepoint.

William George Smith, age 26, convicted of the murder of girlfriend Elizabeth Bousfield. Executed at Hull, 9 December 1924. Hangman: Thomas Pierrepoint.

Arthur Simms, age 25, convicted of the murder of sister-in-law Rosa Armstrong. Executed at Nottingham, 17 December 1924. Hangman: Thomas Pierrepoint.

1925

William Grover Bignell, age 32, convicted of the murder of girlfriend Margaret Legg. Executed at Shepton Mallet, 24 February 1925. Hangman: Thomas Pierrepoint.

William Francis Bressington, age 21, convicted of the murder of Gilbert Caleb Amos. Executed at Bristol, 31 March 1925. Hangman: Thomas Pierrepoint.

George William Barton, age 59, convicted of the murder of sister-in-law Mary Palfrey. Executed at Pentonville, 2 April 1925. Hangman: Robert Baxter.

Henry Graham, age 42, convicted of the murder of wife Margaret. Executed at Durham, 15 April 1925. Hangman: Thomas Pierrepoint.

Thomas Henry Shelton, age 25, convicted of the murder of Ruth Surtees Rodgers. Executed at Durham, 15 April 1925. Hangman: Thomas Pierrepoint.

John Norman Holmes Thorne, age 24, convicted of the murder of girlfriend Elsie Cameron. Executed at Wandsworth, 22 April 1925. Hangman: Thomas Pierrepoint.

Patrick Power, age 41, convicted of the murder of Sarah Ann Sykes. Executed at Manchester, 26 May 1925. Hangman: Thomas Pierrepoint.

Hubert Ernest Dalton, age 39, convicted of the murder of Francis Ward. Executed at Hull, 10 June 1925. Hangman: Thomas Pierrepoint.

James Winstanley, age 29, convicted of the murder of girlfriend Edith Wilkinson. Executed at Liverpool, 5 August 1925. Hangman: William Willis.

James Makin, age 25, convicted of the murder of Sarah Clutton. Executed at Manchester, 11 August 1925. Hangman: Thomas Pierrepoint.

Arthur Henry Bishop, age 18, convicted of the murder of Francis Rix. Executed at Pentonville, 14 August 1925. Hangman: Robert Baxter.

William John Cronin, age 54, convicted of the murder of girlfriend Alice Garnett. Executed at Pentonville, 14 August 1925. Hangman: Robert Baxter.

Alfred Bostock, age 25, convicted of the murder of girlfriend Elizabeth Sherrat. Executed at Leeds, 3 September 1925. Hangman: Thomas Pierrepoint.

William and Lawrence Fowler, ages 23 and 25, jointly convicted of the murder of William F. Plommer. Executed at Leeds, 3 and 4 September 1925. Hangman in both cases was Thomas Pierrepoint.

John Keen, age 22, convicted of the murder of Noorh Mohammed. Executed at Glasgow, 24 September 1925. Hangman: Thomas Pierrepoint.

Herbert George Whiteman, age 27, convicted of the murders of mother-in-law Clara Squires and wife Alice Mabel. Executed at Norwich, 12 November 1925. Hangman: Robert Baxter.

Samuel Johnson, age 29, convicted of the murder of girlfriend Beatrice Philomena Martin. Executed at Manchester, 15 December 1925. Hangman: William Willis.

1926

John Fisher, age 55, convicted of the murder of girlfriend Ada Taylor. Executed at Birmingham, 5 January 1926. Hangman: William Willis.

Lorraine Lax, age 28, convicted of the murder of wife Elizabeth. Executed at Leeds, 7 January 1926. Hangman: Thomas Pierrepoint.

Herbert Burrows, age 23, convicted of the murders of Ernest, Doris and Robert Laight. Executed at Gloucester, 17 February 1926. Hangman: Thomas Pierrepoint.

Probationary policeman Herbert Burrows lived across the street from the Garibaldi Inn, Wylds Lane, Gloucester, and it was here on the night of 27 November 1926 that a burglar shot the landlord and landlady and then battered their 2-year-old son to death. Suspicion soon turned on Burrows when he told colleagues that he had been the last person to see the Laights alive, the Garibaldi Inn being his local, and he revealed details that were not common knowledge even among the local police constables. When detectives searched Burrows' home they found the gun used in the shooting as well as a large sum of cash. The policeman confessed to the crimes, saying he was desperately short of money.

John Lincoln, age 23, convicted of the murder of Edward Charles Richards. Executed at Shepton Mallet. Hangman: Thomas Pierrepoint.

Henry Thompson, age 36, convicted of the murder of girlfriend Rose Smith. Executed at Maidstone, 9 March 1926. Hangman: Thomas Pierrepoint.

George Thomas, age 26, convicted of the murder of girlfriend Marie Beddoe Thomas. Executed at Cardiff, 9 March 1926. Hangman: Robert Baxter.

William Henry Thorpe, age 45, convicted of the murder of girlfriend Frances Clark. Executed at Manchester, 16 March 1926. Hangman: William Willis.

Lock Ah Tam, age 54, convicted of the murders of wife Catherine and daughter Celcilia. Executed at Liverpool, 23 March 1926. Hangman: William Willis.

Ewen Stitchell, age 25, convicted of the murder of Polly Edward Walker. Executed at Pentonville, 24 March 1926. Hangman: Robert Baxter.

George Sharples, age 20, convicted of the murder of Milly Crabtree. Executed at Birmingham, 13 April 1926. Hangman: William Willis.

Louis Calvert, age 33, convicted of the murder of Lily Waterhouse. Executed at Manchester, 24 June 1926. Hangman: Thomas Pierrepoint.

Johannes Josephus Mommers, age 43, convicted of the murder of Augusta Pionbini. Executed at Pentonville, 27 July 1926. Hangman: Robert Baxter.

James Smith, age 23, convicted of the murder of wife Catherine. Executed at Durham, 10 August 1926. Hangman: Thomas Pierrepoint.

Charles Edward Finden, age 22, convicted of the murder of John Richard Thompson. Executed at Winchester, 12 August 1926. Hangman: Thomas Pierrepoint.

Hashankhan Samander, age 36, convicted of the murder of Khannar Jung Baz. Executed at Pentonville, 14 September 1926. Hangman: Robert Baxter.

James Leah, age 60, convicted of the murder of daughter Louise. Executed at Liverpool, 16 November 1926. Hangman: Thomas Pierrepoint.

Charles Houghton, age 45, convicted of the murder of Eleanor and Martha Woodhouse. Executed at Gloucester, 3 December 1926. Hangman: Thomas Pierrepoint.

1927

William Cornelius Jones, age 22, convicted of the murder of wife Winifred. Executed at Leeds, 5 January 1927. Hangman: Thomas Pierrepoint.

James Frederick Stratton, age 26, convicted of the murder of girlfriend Madge Dorothy Maggs. Executed at Pentonville, 29 March 1927. Hangman: Robert Baxter.

William Knighton, age 22, convicted of the murder of mother Ada. Executed at Nottingham, 27 August 1927. Hangman: Thomas Pierrepoint.

Frederick Fuller and James Murphy, ages 35 and 29, jointly convicted of the murder of James Staunton. Executed at Wandsworth, 3 August 1927. Hangman: Robert Baxter.

John Robinson, age 36, convicted of the murder of Minnie Alice Bonati. Executed at Pentonville, 12 August 1927. Hangman: Robert Baxter.

Arthur Harnett, age 28, convicted of the murder of Isabella Moore. Executed at Leeds, 2 September 1927. Hangman: Thomas Pierrepoint.

William Meynell Robertson, age 32, convicted of the murder of girlfriend Evelyn Jenkins. Executed at Liverpool, 6 December 1927. Hangman: Thomas Pierrepoint.

1928

Frederick Fielding, age 24, convicted of the murder of girlfriend Eleanor Pilkington. Executed at Manchester, 3 January 1928. Hangman: Thomas Pierrepoint.

Bertram Horace Kirby, age 47, convicted of the murder of wife Minnie. Executed at Lincoln, 4 January 1928. Hangman: Thomas Pierrepoint.

John Thomas Dunn, age 52, convicted of the murder of wife Ada Elizabeth. Executed at Durham, 6 January 1928. Hangman: Thomas Pierrepoint.

Sidney Bernard Goulter, age 25, convicted of the murder of Constance Oliver. Executed at Wandsworth, 6 January 1928. Hangman: Robert Baxter.

Samuel Case, age 24, convicted of the murder of girlfriend Mary Alice Mottram. Executed at Leeds, 7 January 1928. Hangman: Thomas Pierrepoint.

James McKay, age 40, convicted of the murder of mother Agnes Arbuckle. Executed at Glasgow, 24 January 1928. Hangman: Robert Baxter.

Edward Rowlands and Daniel Driscoll, ages 40 and 34, jointly convicted of the murder of David Lewis. Executed at Cardiff, 27 January 1928. Hangman: Robert Baxter.

James Gillon, age 30, convicted of the murder of sister Annie. Executed at Wandsworth, 31 January 1928. Hangman: Robert Baxter.

John Joseph Gillan, age 32, convicted of the murder of Olive Turner. Executed at Birmingham, 31 January 1928. Hangman: Thomas Pierrepoint.

George Frederick Hayward, age 32, convicted of the murder of Amy Collinson. Executed at Nottingham, 10 April 1928. Hangman: Thomas Pierrepoint.

Frederick Lock, age 39, convicted of the murder of girlfriend Florence Alice Kitching. Executed at Wandsworth, 12 April 1928. Hangman: Robert Baxter.

Frederick Browne and William Kennedy, ages 47 and 36, jointly convicted of the murder of Constable William Gutteridge. Executed at Pentonville, 31 May 1928. Hangmen were Robert Baxter and Thomas Pierrepoint.

The murder of PC Gutteridge was unpleasant, but there is strong evidence that Frederick Browne was actually innocent. It was the morning of 27 September 1927 when Constable William Gutteridge stopped a car that he suspected had been stolen, and while he made to question the driver he was shot twice in the head. Fatally wounded, the policeman fell to the ground only for the killer to emerge from the car and shoot him twice more, putting a bullet into each of his eyes.

The stolen car was traced to the garage of Frederick Browne and when police searched the premises a number of firearms were found. One of these, a Webley, was identified by experts as being the weapon that had killed the police constable. Meanwhile in Liverpool, William Kennedy was arrested in connection with the car theft and he was eager to give a detailed statement in which he admitted being in the stolen car with Browne and had witnessed the shooting of the policeman. By incriminating Browne in the murder Kennedy was aiming to escape the hangman and get a long prison sentence instead.

The jury convicted both men and both were sentenced to death. But Browne strongly protested his innocence and evidence given by his landlady, who said he was at home on the night of the murder, was not put before the court. Both men hanged at exactly the same time.

Frederick Stewart, age 28, convicted of the murder of Alfred Charles Webb. Executed at Pentonville, 6 June 1928. Hangman: Robert Baxter.

Walter Brooks, age 48, convicted of the murders of wife Beatrice and Alfred Moore. Executed at Manchester, 28 June 1928. Hangman: Thomas Pierrepoint.

Albert George Absalom, age 28, convicted of the murder of girlfriend Mary Reed. Executed at Liverpool, 25 July 1928. Hangman: Thomas Pierrepoint.

William John Maynard, age 36, convicted of the murder of Richard Roadley. Executed at Exeter, 27 July 1928. Hangman: Thomas Pierrepoint.

George Reynold, age 41, convicted of the murder of Thomas Lee. Executed at Glasgow, 3 August 1928. Hangman: Robert Baxter.

William Smiley, age 28, convicted of the murders of Margaret and Sarah Macauley. Executed at Belfast, 8 August 1928. Hangman: Thomas Pierrepoint.

Norman Elliott, age 23, convicted of the murder of William Byland Abbey. Executed at Durham, 10 August 1928. Hangman: Thomas Pierrepoint.

Allen Wales, age 22, convicted of the murder of wife Isabella. Executed at Edinburgh, 13 August 1928. Hangman: Robert Baxter.

William Charles Benson, age 25, convicted of the murder of girlfriend Charlotte Alice Harber. Executed at Wandsworth, 20 November 1928. Hangman: Robert Baxter.

Chung Yi Maio, age 28, convicted of the murder of wife Wai Sheung Sui. Executed at Manchester, 6 December 1928. Hangman: Thomas Pierrepoint.

Trevor John Edwards, age 21, convicted of the murder of girlfriend Elsie Cook. Executed at Swansea, 11 December 1928. Hangman: Robert Baxter.

1929

Charles William Conlin, age 22, convicted of the murder of grandparents Thomas and Emily Kirby. Executed at Durham, 4 January 1929. Hangman: Thomas Pierrepoint.

Frederick Hollington, age 25, convicted of the murder of girlfriend Annie Hatton. Executed at Pentonville, 20 February 1929. Hangman: Robert Baxter.

William John Holmyard, age 24, convicted of the murder of grandfather William Holmyard. Executed at Pentonville, 27 February 1929. Hangman: Thomas Pierrepoint.

Joseph Reginald Victor Clarke, age 21, convicted of the murder of Alice Fontaine. Executed at Liverpool, 12 March 1929. Hangman: Thomas Pierrepoint.

George Henry Cartledge, age 29, convicted of the murder of wife Ellen Cartledge. Executed at Manchester, 4 April 1929. Hangman: Thomas Pierrepoint.

James Johnson, age 43, convicted of the murder of wife Mary Annie. Executed at Durham, 7 August 1928. Hangman: Thomas Pierrepoint.

Arthur Leslie Raveney, age 24, convicted of the murder of Leslie White. Executed at Leeds, 14 August 1929. Hangman: Thomas Pierrepoint.

John Maguire, age 43, convicted of the murder of wife Ellen. Executed at Liverpool, 26 November 1929. Hangman: Thomas Pierrepoint.

1930

Sidney Harry Fox, age 31, convicted of the murder of mother Rosaline. Executed at Maidstone, 8 April 1930. Hangman: Robert Baxter.

Samuel Cushnan, age 26, convicted of the murder of James McCann. Executed at Belfast, 8 April 1930. Hangman: Thomas Pierrepoint.

William Henry Podmore, age 29, convicted of the murder of Vivian Messiter. Executed at Winchester, 22 April 1930. Hangman: Thomas Pierrepoint.

It was first class detective work that brought William Henry Podmore to justice. It was a textbook example of how police forces can work together and achieve something that would have been impossible otherwise.

Vivian Messiter was a sales agent for the Wolf's Head Oil Company and he ran his business from a rented storeroom at Grove Street in Southampton. On 30 October 1928 he vanished, seemingly without trace. On 1 November the landlord, a Mr Parrot, went to the storeroom to see Mr Messiter but found that all the storeroom doors were locked. Guessing that Mr Messiter had gone away for a short time, he was not unduly troubled; Messiter after all was a model tenant and seemed a trustworthy gentleman. Eventually the oil company grew concerned and informed police that they had not heard from their sales agent for some time. When the police visited the storerooms they too found them securely locked, but they could see no reason to gain entry. Eventually the oil company had to appoint a new sales agent. It was assumed that Messiter had simply run off and, although this was out of character, such events were not unheard of. Maybe he had met a woman.

The new sales agent, a Mr Passmore, had to force entry into the storerooms and it was then that the mystery of Mr Messiter's disappearance was solved. There, behind a pile of cases, was his body – he seemed to have been shot in one eye.

The post-mortem would reveal that Mr Messiter had been beaten to death. A heavy hammer had been brought down on his head three times, the final blow striking him in the left eye. The eye had been pushed into the skull leaving the appearance of a bullet wound. The police found a receipt book close to the body from which two pages had been torn. The last receipt in the book was dated 30 October 1928. The police now tried to figure out what had been on the two pages that had been torn out of the book. The second missing page had an entry that had left an impression on the page beneath and police could work out the initials: W.F.T.

Carbon sheets were then discovered and these were filled with names that would prove to be fictitious – the deduction was that someone who had been doing business with Mr Messiter, one of the sub-agents most likely, had placed fictitious orders and was claiming commission on these non-sales. If Messiter had found out about this then maybe it was enough to get him killed. It was now vital to find out who W.F.T. was.

The storeroom was searched again, and a scrap of paper was found that contained a note from Messiter to a Mr William F. Thomas. And then when police again searched Messiter's lodgings they found a letter that contained an address for William F. Thomas. The police went to the address in Southampton but Thomas had already left and the forwarding address he had given his landlord turned out to be false.

The police now sent details on Thomas to several other forces and received some interesting replies. Wiltshire police were looking for Thomas for the theft of wage packets from a Salisbury garage. When the police searched Thomas's lodgings in Salisbury they found another scrap of paper carrying the name of Podmore and part of an address in Manchester. The name Podmore was known to police in Manchester, where he was wanted for fraud, and now police were convinced that William F. Thomas and Podmore were one and the same.

The next breakthrough came from the police in Stoke-on-Trent who had also run into Podmore and they were able to share more information. Podmore was known to spend time with a woman named Lily Hambleton and it was believed that she was currently residing at the Leicester Hotel on London's Vauxhall Road. It was here that police finally caught up with William Henry Podmore. Knowing that they had to present as strong a case as possible if they were to charge Podmore with murder, the police decided to transfer him to Manchester to face the fraud charges. Here he was sentenced to three months; time the police would spend building their case against him for the murder of Mr Messiter.

On his release, Podmore was immediately arrested and transferred to Winchester to face charges of theft, and he found himself serving another six-month sentence. And then when he was released he was arrested again and this time charged with the murder of Vivian Messiter. The police had been able to link the false names on the carbon papers to people Podmore had known, and even to streets around where he had lived as a child. They were also able to prove that he had borrowed a hammer, of the same type used to kill Mr Messiter, from a friend in the motor trade. Podmore, faced with the evidence, admitted that he had been with Mr Messiter on the day he had been killed, but claimed that the man was alive when they parted.

His murder trial lasted five days before the jury brought in a unanimous verdict of guilty, and so, eighteen months after the murder of Vivian Messiter, and thanks to an exemplary police investigation, the killer faced the hangman.

Albert Edward Marjeram, age 23, convicted of the murder of Edith May Parker. Executed at Wandsworth, 11 June 1930. Hangman: Thomas Pierrepoint.

1931

Victor Edward Betts, age 21, convicted of the murder of William Andrews. Executed at Birmingham, 3 January 1931. Hangman: Thomas Pierrepoint.

Frederick Gill, age 26, convicted of the murder of Oliver Preston. Executed at Leeds, 4 February 1931. Hangman: Thomas Pierrepoint.

Alfred Arthur Rouse, age 36, convicted of the murder of unidentified male. Executed at Bedford, 10 March 1931. Hangman: Thomas Pierrepoint.

Alfred Rouse was a man with an eye for the ladies and they seemed to like him too, which caused his problems when a string of affairs meant that children had been born to him up and down the country. By 1931 Rouse was paying more than half his annual wages in maintenance and a way out of this, Rouse figured, was to fake his own death. To this end Rouse befriended a drunken down-and-out in a pub in Whetstone and drove him in his car to a lane in Northamptonshire. Here Rouse knocked the man unconscious, placed him in the driver's seat, and then doused the vehicle with petrol. Then Rouse threw a match into the car and watched as it became a furnace, knowing the unfortunate man would be so badly burned that the authorities would take it for himself. But, despite it being after two in the morning, two local men saw him as he made his escape. He now knew that his plan had failed. Rouse faced the hangman and the charred corpse in his car was never identified.

Francis Land, age 39, convicted of the murder of girlfriend Sarah Johnson. Executed at Manchester, 16 April 1931. Hangman: Thomas Pierrepoint.

Alexander Anastassiou, age 23, convicted of the murder of girlfriend Evelyn Holt. Executed at Pentonville, 3 June 1931. Hangman: Robert Baxter.

Thomas Dornan, age not recorded in court records, convicted of the murders of sisters Isabella and Margaret Aitkin. Executed at Belfast, 31 July 1931. Hangman: Thomas Pierrepoint.

William Shelley and Oliver Newman, ages 57 and 61, jointly convicted of the murder of Herbert William. Executed at Pentonville, 5 August 1931. Hangman: Robert Baxter.

William John Corbett, age 32, convicted of the murder of wife Ethel Corbett. Executed at Cardiff. The identity of the hangman is not recorded in court records.

Henry Seymour, age 39, convicted of the murder of Alice Kempson. Executed at Oxford, 10 December 1931. The identity of the hangman is not recorded in court records.

Solomon Stein, age 21, convicted of the murder of Annie Riley. Executed at Manchester, 15 December 1931. Hangman: Thomas Pierrepoint.

1932

Eddie Cullins, age 26, convicted of the murder of Achmet Musa. Executed at Belfast, 13 January 1932. Hangman: Thomas Pierrepoint.

George Alfred Rice, age 32, convicted of the murder of Constance Inman. Executed at Manchester, 3 February 1932. Hangman: Thomas Pierrepoint.

William Harold Goddard, age 25, convicted of the murder of Charles William Lambert. Executed at Pentonville, 23 February 1932. Hangman: Robert Baxter.

George Thomas Pople, age 22, convicted of the murder of Mabel Mathews. Executed at Oxford, 9 March 1932. The identity of the hangman is not recorded in court records.

George Michael, age 49, convicted of the murder of girlfriend Theresa Hempstock. Executed at Hull, 27 April 1932. Hangman: Thomas Pierrepoint.

Thomas Riley, age 36, convicted of the murder of girlfriend Elizabeth Castle. Executed at Leeds, 28 April 1932. Hangman: Thomas Pierrepoint.

John Henry Roberts, age 23, convicted of the murder of Alfred Gill. Executed at Leeds, 28 April 1932. Hangman: Thomas Pierrepoint.

Maurice Freedman, age 36, convicted of the murder of girlfriend Annette Friedson. Executed at Pentonville, 4 May 1932. Hangman: Robert Baxter.

Charles James Cowle, age 19, convicted of the murder of Naomi Farnworth. Executed at Manchester, 18 May 1932. Hangman: Thomas Pierrepoint.

Ernest Hutchinson, age 43, convicted of the murder of girlfriend Gwendoline Warren. Executed at Oxford, 23 November 1932. Hangman: Robert Baxter.

1933

Jeremiah Hanbury, age 49, convicted of the murder of girlfriend Jessie Payne. Executed at Birmingham, 2 February 1933. Hangman: Thomas Pierrepoint.

During this execution, Albert Pierrepoint, soon to be the most famous hangman of them all, served as assistant to his uncle Thomas. This was the first time Albert worked as an official hangman's assistant.

Jack Samuel Puttnam, age 31, convicted of the murder of aunt Elizabeth Standley. Executed at Pentonville, 8 June 1933. Hangman: Robert Baxter.

Richard Hetherington, age 36, convicted of the murders of Joseph and Mary Nixon. Executed at Liverpool, 20 June 1933. Hangman: Thomas Pierrepoint.

Frederick Morse, age 34, convicted of the murder of Doris Brewer. Executed at Bristol, 25 July 1933. Hangman: Thomas Pierrepoint.

Vernavas Antorka, age 31, convicted of the murder of Boleslar Pankorski. Executed at Pentonville, 10 August 1933. Hangman: Robert Baxter.

Robert James Kirby, age 26, convicted of the murder of girlfriend Grace Newing. Executed at Pentonville, 11 October 1933. Hangman: Robert Baxter.

Ernest Wedge Parker, age 25, convicted of the murder of sister Lily. Executed at Durham, 6 December 1933. Hangman: Thomas Pierrepoint.

William Burtoft, age 47, convicted of the murder of Francis Levin. Executed at Manchester, 19 December 1933. Hangman: Thomas Pierrepoint.

Stanley Eric Hobday, age 21, convicted of the murder of Charles William Fox. Executed at Birmingham, 28 December 1933. Hangman: Thomas Pierrepoint.

MR. CHARLES DICKENS AND THE EXECUTION OF THE MANNINGS.

MR. EDITOR,—I was a witness of the execution at Horsemonger-lane. I went there with the intention of observing the crowd gathered to behold it, and I had excellent opportunities of doing so, at intervals all through the night, and continuously from daybreak until after the spectacle was over. I do not address you on the subject with any intention of discussing the abstract question of capital punishment, or any of the arguments of its opponents or advocates. I simply wish to turn this dreadful experience to some account for the general good, by taking the readiest and most public means of adverting to an intimation given by Sir G. Grey in the last Session of Parliament, that the Government might be induced to give its support to a measure making the infliction of capital punishment a private solemnity within the prison walls (with such guarantees for the last sentence of the law being inexorably and surely administered as should be satisfactory to the public at large), and of most earnestly beseeching Sir G. Grey, as a solemn duty which he owes to society, and a responsibility which he cannot for ever put away, to originate such a legislative change himself.

I believe that a sight so inconceivably awful as the wickedness and levity of the immense crowd collected at that execution could be imagined by no man, and could be presented in no heathen land under the sun. The horrors of the gibbet and of the crime which brought the wretched murderers to it, faded in my mind before the atrocious bearing, looks and language, of the assembled spectators. When I came upon the scene at midnight, the *shrillness* of the cries and howls that were raised from time to time, denoting that they came from a concourse of boys and girls already assembled in the best places, made my blood run cold. As the night went on, screeching and laughing, and yelling in strong chorus of parodies on negro melodies, with substitutions of 'Mrs. Manning' for 'Susannah,' and the like, were added to these. When the day dawned, thieves, low prostitutes, ruffians and vagabonds of every kind, flocked on to the ground, with every variety of offensive and foul behaviour. Fightings, faintings, whistlings, imitations of Punch, brutal jokes, tumultuous demonstrations of indecent delight when swooning women were dragged out of the crowd by the police with their dresses disordered, gave a new zest to the general entertainment. When the sun rose brightly—as it did—it gilded thousands upon thousands of upturned faces, so inexpressibly odious in their brutal mirth or callousness, that a man had cause to feel ashamed of the shape he wore, and to shrink from himself, as fashioned in the image of the Devil. When the two miserable creatures who attracted all this ghastly sight about them were turned quivering into the air, there was no more emotion, no more pity, no more thought that two immortal souls had gone to judgment, no more restraint in any of the previous obscenities, than if the name of Christ had never been heard in this world, and there were no belief among men but that they perished like the beasts. I have seen, habitually, some of the worst sources of general contamination and corruption in this country, and I think there are not many phases of London life that could surprise me. I am solemnly convinced that nothing that ingenuity could devise to be done in this city, in the same compass of time, could work such ruin as one public execution, and I stand astounded and appalled by the wickedness it exhibits. I do not believe that any community can prosper where such a scene of horror and demoralization as was enacted outside Horsemonger-lane Jail is presented at the very doors of good citizens, and is passed by, unknown or forgotten. And when, in our prayers and thanksgivings for the season, we are humbly expressing before God our desire to remove the moral evils of the land, I would ask your readers to consider whether it is not a time to think of this one, and to root it out.

I am, Sir, your faithful servant,
CHARLES DICKENS.

Devonshire-terrace, Tuesday, Nov. 13.

Right: Letter from Charles Dickens to *The Times* describing a public hanging he had observed.

Below: Witches being hung.

A public execution at Tower Hill.

A mass hanging at Tyburn, 1772.

Lord Aberdare, who led the Aberdare Committee to modernise capital punishment.

Above left: Timothy Evans was wrongly executed.

Above right: William Calcraft.

Below: Gwynne Evans and Peter Allan were the last men to be hanged in the United Kingdom.

Albert Pierrepoint.

As well as being Britain's best known hangman, Albert Pierrepoint was also the smiling landlord of his own club.

Henry Allen was the United Kingdom's last hangman.

William Calcraft   William Marwood   James Berry   James Billington   Henry Pierrepoint

John Ellis   Thomas Pierrepoint   Albert Pierrepoint   Harry Allen   Leslie Stewart

Above: British hangmen.

Below: Ruth Ellis and David Blakely.

POST MORTEM EXAMINATION

Name Ellis, Ruth Apparent Age 28 years

At H. M. Prison Holloway Date July 13 1955

EXTERNAL EXAMINATION	Well nourished Evidence of proper care and attention. Height 5ft. 2ins. Weight 103 lbs.
	DEEP IMPRESSIONS AROUND NECK from noose with a suspension point about 1 inch in front of the angle of the L. lower jaw. Vital changes locally and in the tissues beneath as a consequence of sudden constriction. No ecchymoses in the face, or indeed, elsewhere. No marks of restraint. 1 hour.
How long dead	
INTERNAL EXAMINATION	
Skull	Fracture - dislocation of the spine at C2 with a 2 inch gap and transverse separation of the spinal cord at the same level.
Basic Meninges	
Mouth, tongue, Oesophagus	Fracture of both wings of the Hyoid and R. wing of the Thyroid cartilage, larynx also fractured.
Larynx, Trachea, Lungs	Air passages clear and lungs quite free from disease or other change. No engorgement. No asphyxial changes.
Pericardium, Heart and blood vessels	No organic changes. No petechiae or other evidence of organic change. Small food residue, and odour of brandy. No disease.
Stomach and contents ...	
Peritoneum Intestines, etc. ...	Normal. Terminal congestion only.
Liver, and Gall bladder	Normal.
Spleen.	Slight terminal congestion only.
Kidneys and Ureters Bladder etc.	Lower abdominal operation scar for ectopic pregnancy operation in L. tube, now healed. No pregnancy.
Generative organs	
Other remarks _ ...	Deceased was a healthy subject at the time of death.

Ruth Ellis' post-mortem report.

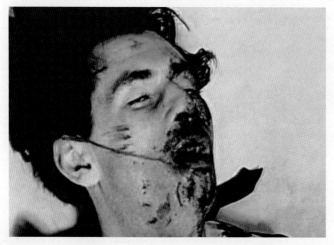

Police photograph showing David Blakely following his shooting.

Crowds gather outside Holloway Prison to protest the execution of Ruth Ellis.

Above: Noose

Right: Noted abolitionist
Mrs Violet Van der Elst.

Derek Bentley, who was hanged for a crime committed by another.

Above left: James Berry was the first British hangman to publish his memoirs.

Above right: William Joyce (Lord Haw Haw), was hanged at Wandsworth by Albert Pierrepoint.

1934

Roy Gregory, age 28, convicted of the murder of stepdaughter Dorothy Addinall. Executed at Hull, 3 January 1934. Hangman: Thomas Pierrepoint.

Ernest Brown, age 35, convicted of the murder of Frederick Morton. Executed at Leeds, 6 February 1934. Hangman: Thomas Pierrepoint.

Louis Hamilton, age 25, convicted of the murder of wife Maud Hamilton. Executed at Leeds, 6 April 1934. Hangman: Thomas Pierrepoint.

Reginald Ivor Hinks, age 32, convicted of the murder of father-in-law James Pullen. Executed at Bristol, 3 May 1934. Hangman: Thomas Pierrepoint.

Albert Probert and Frederick Williams, ages 26 and 21, jointly convicted of the murder of Joseph Bedford. Executed at Wandsworth, 4 May 1934. Hangman: Thomas Pierrepoint.

Harry Tuffney, age 36, convicted of the murder of girlfriend Edith Longshaw. Executed at Pentonville, 9 October 1934. Hangman: Robert Baxter.

John Frederick Stockwell, age 19, convicted of the murder of Dudley Hoard. Executed at Pentonville, 14 November 1934. Hangman: Robert Baxter.

Ethel Lillie Major, age 42, convicted of the murder of husband, Arthur Major. Executed at Hull, 19 December 1934. Hangman: Thomas Pierrepoint.

1935

Frederick Rushworth, age 29, convicted of the murder of unnamed infant daughter. Executed at Leeds, 1 January 1935. Hangman: Thomas Pierrepoint.

David Maskill Blake, 24, convicted of the murder of Emily Yeomans. Executed at Leeds, 7 February 1935. Hangman: Thomas Pierrepoint.

Charles Malcolm Lake, age 37, convicted of the murder of George Hamilton. Executed at Pentonville, 13 March 1939. Hangman: Robert Baxter.

Leonard Albert Brigstock, age 33, convicted of the murder of Hubert Sidney Deggan. Executed at Wandsworth, 2 April 1935. Hangman: Robert Baxter.

Percy Anderson, age 21, convicted of the murder of girlfriend Edith Constance Bear, executed at Wandsworth, 16 April 1935. Hangman: Thomas Pierrepoint.

John Bainbridge, age 24, convicted of the murder of Edward Herdman. Executed at Durham, 9 May 1935. The identity of the hangman is not recorded in court records.

John Harris Bridge, age 25, convicted of the murder of girlfriend Amelia Nuttal. Executed at Manchester, 30 May 1935. Hangman: Thomas Pierrepoint.

Arthur Henry Franklin, age 44, convicted of the murder of girlfriend Bessie Gladys Nott. Executed at Gloucester, 25 June 1935. Hangman: Thomas Pierrepoint.

Allan James Grierson, age 27, convicted of the murder of Louise Berthe Gann. Executed at Pentonville, 30 October 1935. Hangman: Robert Baxter.

1936

Dorothy Waddington, age 36, convicted of the murders of Louisa and Ada Baguley. Executed at Birmingham, 16 April 1936. Hangman: Thomas Pierrepoint.

Bukhtyar Rustomji Hakin, age 36, convicted of the murders of Isabella Ess and Mary Rogerson. Executed at Manchester, 12 May 1936. Hangman: Thomas Pierrepoint.

Frederick Charles Field, age 32, convicted of the murder of Beatrice Sutton. Executed at Wandsworth, 30 June 1936. Hangman: Alfred Allen.

George Arthur Bryant, convicted of the murder of girlfriend Ellen Mary Whiting. Executed at Wandsworth, 14 July 1936. Hangman: Thomas Pierrepoint.

Charlotte Bryant, age 33, convicted of the murder of husband Frederick. Executed at Exeter, 15 July 1936. Hangman: Thomas Pierrepoint.

Wallace Johnson, age 57, convicted of the murder of girlfriend Alice Whye. Executed at Wandsworth, 5 August 1936. Hangman: Thomas Pierrepoint.

Christopher Jackson, age 24, convicted of the murder of aunt Harriet May Linney. Executed at Durham, 16 December 1936. Hangman: Thomas Pierrepoint.

1937

Max Haslam, age 23, convicted of the murder of Ruth Clarkson. Executed at Manchester, 4 February 1937. Hangman: Thomas Pierrepoint.

Andrew Anderson Bagley, age 62, convicted of the murder of Irene Hart. Executed at Leeds, 10 February 1937. Hangman: Thomas Pierrepoint.

Philip Edward Percy Davies, age 30, convicted of the murders of wife Wilhelmina and niece Monica Rowe. Executed at Exeter, 27 July 1937. Hangman: Thomas Pierrepoint.

Horace William Brunt, age 32, convicted of the murder of Kate Collier. Executed at Manchester, 12 August 1937. The identity of the hangman is not recorded.

Leslie George Stone, age 24, convicted of the murder of girlfriend Ruby Ann Keen. Executed at Pentonville, 13 August 1937. Hangman: Thomas Pierrepoint.

Frederick George Murphy, age 53, convicted of the murder of Rosina Field. Executed at Pentonville, 17 August 1937. Hangman: Alfred Allen.

John Thomas Rogers, age 22, convicted of the murder of Lilian Chamberlain. Executed at Pentonville, 18 November 1937. Hangman: Thomas Pierrepoint.

Ernest John Moss, age 28, convicted of the murder of girlfriend Kitty Bennett. Executed at Exeter, 7 December 1937. Hangman: Thomas Pierrepoint.

Frederick Nodder, age 44, convicted of the murder of Mona Lilian Tinsley. Executed at Lincoln, 30 December 1937. The identity of the hangman is not recorded, but is likely to have been Thomas Pierrepoint.

1938

Walter Smith, age 33, convicted of the murder of Albert Edward Baker. Executed at Norwich, 8 March 1928. Hangman: Thomas Pierrepoint.

Charles James Caldwell, age 49, convicted of the murder of wife Eliza Caldwell. Executed at Manchester, 20 April 1938. The identity of the hangman is not recorded.

Robert William Hoolhouse, age 21, convicted of the murder of Margaret Jane Dobson. Executed at Durham, 26 May 1938. Hangman: Thomas Pierrepoint.

Jan Mohamed, age 30, convicted of the murder of Aminul Hag. Executed at Liverpool, 8 June 1938. The identity of the hangman is not recorded.

Alfred Ernest Richards, age 38, convicted of the murder of wife Kathleen Richards. Executed at Wandsworth, 12 July 1938. Hangman: Thomas Pierrepoint.

William Graves, age 38, convicted of the murder of infant son Tony Ruffle. Executed at Wandsworth, 19 July 1938. Hangman: Thomas Pierrepoint.

William Parker, age 25, convicted of the killing of wife Jane Ann Parker. Executed at Durham, 26 July 1938. Hangman: Thomas Pierrepoint.
    William Parker claimed to have strangled his wife because she killed, by strangulation, their two children, Theresa and Cecil. However the court preferred to believe that it had been Parker who had killed all three members of his family; but he was only convicted and hanged for the murder of his wife.

George Brains, age 27, convicted of the murder of Rose Atkins. Executed at Wandsworth, 1 November 1938. Hangman: Thomas Pierrepoint.

1939

John Daymond, age 19, convicted of the murder of James Percival. Executed at Durham, 8 February 1939. Hangman: Thomas Pierrepoint.

Harry Armstrong, age 38, convicted of the murder of girlfriend Peggy Irene Pentecost. Executed at Wandsworth, 21 March 1939. Hangman: Thomas Pierrepoint.

William Butler, age 29, convicted of the murder of Ernest Key. Executed at Wandsworth, 29 March 1929. Hangman: Thomas Pierrepoint.

Ralph Smith, age 40, convicted of the murder of girlfriend Beatrice Delia Baxter. Executed at Gloucester, 7 June 1939. Hangman: Thomas Pierrepoint.

Leonard Hucker, age 30, convicted of the murder of Mary Alice Maud. Executed at Wandsworth, 10 October 1939. Hangman: Thomas Pierrepoint.

Stanley Ernest Book and Arthur John Smith, aged 27 and 26. Jointly convicted of the murder of Mabel Maud Bundy. Executed at Wandsworth 25 and 26 October 1939. Hangman: Thomas Pierrepoint.

Stanley was hung on 25 October 1939 and one day later John was hanged on the same scaffold.

1940

Peter Barnes and James Richards, aged 32 and 29, jointly convicted of the murders of Elsie Ansell, Gwilym Rowland, John Corbett, James Clay and Rex Gentle. Executed at Birmingham, 7 February 1940. Hangman: Thomas Pierrepoint.

On 25 August 1939 a bomb went off in Broadgate, Coventry, killing five people and leaving another fifty injured. Peter Barnes and James Richards, both having links to the IRA, were arrested and convicted of terrorism.

Ernest Edmund Hamerton, age 25, convicted of the murder of girlfriend Elsie May Ellington. Executed at Wandsworth, 27 March 1940. Hangman: Thomas Phillips.

William Charles Cowell, 38, convicted of the murder of Anne Farrow Cook. Executed at Wandsworth, 24 April 1940. Hangman: Thomas Pierrepoint.

Vincent Ostler and William Appleby, ages 24 and 27, jointly convicted of the murder of William Ralph Shiell. Executed at Durham, 11 July 1940. Hangman: Thomas Pierrepoint.

Udham Smith, age 37, convicted of the murder of Sir Michael O'Dwyer. Executed at Pentonville, 31 July 1940. Hangman: Stanley Cross.

George Edward Roberts, age 29, convicted of the murder of Arthur John Allen. Executed at Cardiff, 8 August 1940. The identity of the hangman is not recorded.

John William Wright, age 41, convicted of the murder of wife Alice Wright. Executed at Durham, 10 September 1940. Hangman: Thomas Pierrepoint.

Stanley Cole, age 23, convicted of the murder of Doris Eugenia Girl. Executed at Wandsworth, 31 October 1940. Hangman: Thomas Pierrepoint.

William Henry Cooper, age 24, convicted of the murder of John Joseph Harrison. Executed at Bedford, 26 November 1940. Hangman: Thomas Pierrepoint.

John Waldeburg and Carl Meler, ages 25 and 24. Convicted of spying. Executed at Pentonville, 10 December 1940. Hangman: Stanley Cross.

Charles Albert Van Dem Kieboom, age 26, convicted of spying. Executed at Pentonville, 17 December 1940. Hangman: Stanley Cross.

Edward Scoller, age 42, convicted of the murder of wife Beatrice. Executed at Durham, 24 December 1940. Hangman: Thomas Pierrepoint.

1941

Clifford Holmes, age 24, convicted of the murder of wife Irene Holmes. Executed at Manchester, 11 February 1941. The identity of the hangman is not recorded.

Henry Lyndo White, age 39, convicted of the murder of girlfriend Emily Wardle. Executed at Durham, 6 March 1941. Hangman: Thomas Pierrepoint.

Samuel Morgan, age 28, convicted of the murder of Mary Hagan. Executed at Liverpool, 9 April 1941. Hangman: Thomas Pierrepoint.

George Armstrong, age 39, convicted of spying. Executed at Wandsworth, 9 July 1941. Hangman: Thomas Pierrepoint.

David Miller Jennings, age 21, convicted of the murder of Albert Farley. Executed at Dorchester, 24 July 1941. Hangman: Thomas Pierrepoint.

Edward Walker Anderson, age 19, convicted of the murder of uncle, William Anderson. Executed at Durham, 31 July 1941. Hangman: Thomas Pierrepoint.

Karl Theodore Drucke and Werner Heinrich, ages 25 and 34. Convicted of spying. Executed at Wandsworth, 6 August 1941. Hangman: Thomas Pierrepoint.

Josef Jakobs, age 43, convicted of spying. Executed by firing squad at the Tower of London, 14 August 1941.

  Josef Jakobs made history by being the only man executed by firing squad at the Tower of London in the Second World War.

John Smith, age 32, convicted of the murder of girlfriend Margaret Knight. Executed at Manchester, 4 September 1941. Hangman: Thomas Pierrepoint.

Eli Richards, age 45, convicted of the murder of Jane Turner. Executed at Birmingham, 19 September 1941. Hangman: Thomas Pierrepoint.

Antonio Mancini, age 39, convicted of the murder of Harry Distleman. Executed at Pentonville, 31 October 1941. Hangman: Albert Pierrepoint.

  Although he had assisted in several executions, this was the first time Albert Pierrepoint had taken the role of chief hangman.

Lionel Watson, age 30, convicted of the murders of wife (bigamous) and daughter, Phyllis Elizabeth and Alice Crooker. Executed at Pentonville, 12 November 1941. Hangman: Thomas Pierrepoint.

John Ernest Smith, age 21, convicted of the murder of girlfriend Christina Dicksee. Executed at Wandsworth, 3 December 1941. Hangman: Albert Pierrepoint.

Karl Richard Richter, age 29, convicted of spying. Executed at Wandsworth, 10 December 1941. Hangman: Albert Pierrepoint.

Thomas William Thorpe, age 61, convicted of the murder of wife Nellie. Executed at Leicester, 23 December 1941. Hangman: Thomas Pierrepoint.

1942

Arthur Peach, age 23, convicted of the murder of Kitty Lyon. Executed at Birmingham, 30 January 1941. Hangman: Thomas Pierrepoint.

Harold Trevor, age 62, convicted of the murder of Theodora Greenhill. Executed at Wandsworth, 11 March 1942. Hangman: Albert Pierrepoint.

David Rodger Williams, age 33, convicted of the murder of girlfriend Elizabeth Smith. Executed at Liverpool, 25 March 1942. Hangman: Albert Pierrepoint.

Cyril Johnson, age 20, convicted of the murder of Maggie Small. Executed at Wandsworth, 15 April 1942. Hangman: Thomas Pierrepoint.

Frederick Austin, age 28, convicted of the murder of wife Lilian. Executed at Bristol, 30 April 1942. The identity of the Hangman is not recorded.

Harold Hill, age 26, convicted of the murders of Doreen Joyce and Kathleen Trundell. Executed at Oxford, 1 May 1942. The identity of the hangman is not recorded.

Douglas Edmondson, age 26, convicted of the murder of girlfriend Imeldred Osliff. Executed at Liverpool, 24 June 1942. The identity of the hangman is not recorded.

Gordon Frederick Cummins, age 28, convicted of the murders of Evelyn Hamilton, Evelyn Oatley, Margaret Florance Lowe and Evelyn Oatley. Executed at Wandsworth, 25 June 1942. Hangman: Albert Pierrepoint.
    Were the newspapers not filled with the latest war stories, then it is possible that the name George Frederick Cummins would be as infamous as that of Jack the Ripper. For where the Ripper killed five women in the space of four months, Cummings killed four in the space of a week, and like Jack before him, his victims were prostitutes. Several of his victims were hideously mutilated as though Cummings were styling himself as a latter-day Ripper.

Jose Kay and Alphonso Timmerman, ages 34 and 28, convicted of spying. Executed at Wandsworth, 7 July 1941. Hangman: Albert Pierrepoint.

Arthur Anderson, age 52, convicted of the murder of girlfriend Pauline Barker. Executed at Wandsworth, 21 July 1942. Hangman: Albert Pierrepoint.

Thomas Williams, age 19, convicted of the murder of Patrick Murphy. Executed at Belfast, 2 September 1942. Hangman: Thomas Pierrepoint.

Harold Merry, age 40, convicted of the murder of girlfriend Joyce Dixon. Executed at Birmingham, 10 September 1942. Hangman: Thomas Pierrepoint.

Samuel Dashwood and George Silverosa, aged 23 and 22, jointly convicted of the murder of Leonard Moles. Executed at Pentonville, 10 September 1942. Hangman: Albert Pierrepoint.

Patrick Kingston, age 38, convicted of the murder of Sheila Wilson. Executed at Wandsworth, 6 October 1942. Hangman: Albert Pierrepoint.

William Collins, age 21, convicted of the murder of Margaret Rice. Executed at Durham, 28 October 1942. Hangman: Thomas Pierrepoint.

Duncan Alexander Scott-Ford, age 21, convicted of spying. Executed at Wandsworth, 3 November 1942. Hangman: Albert Pierrepoint.

Herbert Hirman Bounds, age 42, convicted of the murder of wife Elizabeth Bounds. Executed at Wandsworth, 6 November 1942. Hangman: Thomas Pierrepoint.

Johannes Dronkers, age 46, convicted of spying. Executed at Wandsworth, 31 December 1942. Hangman: Albert Pierrepoint.

1943

Francis Winter, age 40, convicted of spying. Executed at Wandsworth, 26 January 1943. Hangman: Albert Pierrepoint.

Harry Dobkin, age 49, convicted of the murder of wife Rachel. Executed at Wandsworth, 27 January 1943. Hangman: Albert Pierrepoint.

Ronald Robert, age 28, convicted of the murder of Nellie Pearson. Executed at Liverpool, 10 February 1943. Hangman: Thomas Pierrepoint.

David Cobb, age 21, convicted of the murder of Robert Cobner. Executed at Shepton Mallet, 12 March 1943. The identity of the hangman is not recorded.

William Henry Turner, age 19, convicted of the murder of Ann Wade. Executed at Pentonville, 24 March 1943. Hangman: Thomas Pierrepoint.

Dudley Rayner, age 26, convicted of the murder of wife Josephine. Executed at Wandsworth, 31 March 1943. Hangman: Albert Pierrepoint.

Gordon Trenoweth, age 33, convicted of the murder of Albert Bateman. Executed at Exeter, 6 April 1943. Hangman: Thomas Pierrepoint.

August Sangret, age 30, convicted of the murder of girlfriend Joan Wolfe. Executed at Wandsworth, 29 April 1943. Hangman: Albert Pierrepoint.

Harold A. Smith, age not recorded, convicted of the murder of Harry Jenkins. Executed at Shepton Mallet, 25 June 1943. The identity of the hangman is not recorded.

Charles Arthur Raymond, age 23, convicted of the murder of Marguerite Burge. Executed at Wandsworth, 10 July 1943. Hangman: Thomas Pierrepoint.

William Quayle, age 52, convicted of the murder of Vera Clarke. Executed at Birmingham, 3 August 1943. Hangman: Thomas Pierrepoint.

Gerald Elphinstone Roe, age 41, convicted of the murder of wife Elsie Elphinstone Roe. Executed at Pentonville, 3 August 1943. Hangman: Albert Pierrepoint.

Thomas Elvin, age 21, convicted of the murder of girlfriend Violet Wakefield. Executed at Leeds, 10 September 1943. Hangman: Thomas Pierrepoint.

Charles Gauthier, age 25, convicted of the murder of girlfriend Annette Pepper. Executed at Wandsworth, 24 September 1943. Hangman: Albert Pierrepoint.

Terence Casey, age 22, convicted of the murder of Bridget Mitton. Executed at Wandsworth, 19 November 1943. Hangman: Albert Pierrepoint.

Lee A. Davies, age not recorded, convicted of the murder of Cynthia Lay. Executed at Shepton Mallet, 14 December 1943. Hangman: Albert Pierrepoint.

Charles William Koopman, age 23, convicted of the murders of Gladys and Shirley Brewer. Executed at Pentonville,15 December 1943. Hangman: Thomas Pierrepoint.

James Dorgan, age 47, convicted of the murder of wife Florence. Executed at Wandsworth, 22 December 1943. Hangman: Thomas Pierrepoint.

Thomas James, age 26, convicted of the murder of Gwendoline Sweeney. Executed at Liverpool, 29 December 1943. The identity of the hangman is not recorded.

1944

Charles Georghiou, age 37, convicted of the murder of Savvas Demetriades. Executed at Pentonville, 2 Febuary 1944. Hangman: Albert Pierrepoint.

Marvin McEwan, age 35, convicted of the murder of Mark Turner. Executed at Leeds, 3 February 1944. Hangman: Thomas Pierrepoint.

John Waters, age 39, convicted of the murder of girlfriend Doris Staples. Executed at Shepton Mallet, 10 February 1944. Hangman: Albert Pierrepoint.

Oswald John Job, age 58, convicted of spying. Executed at Pentonville, 16 March 1944. Hangman: Albert Pierrepoint.

Ernest Digby, age 34, convicted of the murder of infant daughter Dawn. Executed at Bristol, 16 March 1944. The identity of the hangman is not recorded.

J.C. Leatherberry, age not recorded, convicted of the murder of Henry Hailstone. Executed at Shepton Mallet, 16 March 1944. The identity of the hangman is not recorded.

Sidney Delasalle, age 39, convicted of the murder of Ronald Murphy. Executed at Durham, 13 April 1944. Hangman: Albert Pierrepoint.

Wiley Harris, age not recorded, convicted of the murder of Harry Coogan. Executed at Shepton Mallet, 26 May 1944. The identity of the hangman is not recorded.

Alex F. Miranda, age 20, convicted of the murder of Thomas Evison and court martialled. Executed by firing squad at Shepton Mallet.

Ernest James Kemp, age 21, convicted of the murder of Iris Deeley. Convicted of the murder of Iris Deeley. Executed at Wandsworth, 6 June 1944. Hangman: Albert Pierrepoint.

Pierre Neukermans, age 28, convicted of spying. Executed at Pentonville, 23 June 1944. Hangman: Albert Pierrepoint.

Joseph Van Hove, age 27, convicted of spying. Executed at Pentonville, 12 July 1944. Hangman: Albert Pierrepoint.

John Davidson, age 19, convicted of the murder of Gladys Appleton. Executed at Liverpool, 12 July 1944. The identity of the hangman is not recorded.

James Galbraith, age 26, convicted of the murder of James Percey. Executed at Manchester, 26 July 1944. The identity of the hangman is not recorded.

William Alfred Cowle, age 32, convicted of the murder of girlfriend Nora Payne. Executed at Leicester, 8 August 1944. Hangman: Albert Pierrepoint.

William Meffen, age 52, convicted of the murder of stepdaughter Winfred Stanley. Executed at Leicester, 8 August 1944. Hangman: Albert Pierrepoint.

Eliga Brinson and Willie Smith, ages not recorded, convicted of rape. Executed at Shepton Mallet and tried by court martial. Hangman: Albert Pierrepoint.

Madison Thomas, age not recorded, convicted of rape and tried by court martial. Executed at Shepton Mallet, 12 October 1944. The identity of the hangman is not recorded.

Benjamin Pyegate, age not recorded, convicted of the murder of James Alexander and tried by court martial. Executed at Shepton Mallet by firing squad.

Ernest Lee Clark and Augustine Guerra, ages not recorded, convicted of the murder of Elizabeth Green. Executed at Shepton Mallet, 8 December 1944. The identity of the hangman is not recorded.

1945

Horace Beresford Gordon, age 28, convicted of the murder of Dorothy Hillman. Executed at Wandsworth, 9 January 1945. Hangman: Albert Pierrepoint.

Andrew Brown, age 26, convicted of the murder of Amelia Knowles. Executed at Wandsworth, 30 January 1945. Hangman: Albert Pierrepoint.

Arthur Thompson, age 34, convicted of the murder of Jane Coulton. Executed at Leeds, 31 January 1945. Hangman: Thomas Pierrepoint.

Karl Gustav Hulten, age 22, convicted of the murder of George Heath. Executed at Pentonville, 8 March 1945. Hangman: Albert Pierrepoint.

Arthur Hays, age 37, convicted of the murder of Winifred Evans. Executed at Norwich, 13 March 1945. The identity of the hangman is not recorded.

Robert Pearson and Parson Jones, ages not recorded, jointly convicted of rape and tried by court martial. Executed at Shepton Mallet. The identity of the hangman is not recorded.

William Harrison, age not recorded, convicted of the murder of Patricia Wylie and tried by court martial. Executed at Shepton Mallet, 7 April 1945. The identity of the hangman is not recorded.

George E. Smith, age not recorded, convicted of the murder of Eric Teichman and tried by court martial. Executed at Shepton Mallet, 8 May 1945. The identity of the hangman is not recorded.

Aniceto Martinez, age not recorded, convicted of rape and tried by court martial. Executed at Shepton Mallet, 15 June 1945. The identity of the hangman is not recorded.

Howard Joseph Grossley, age 37, convicted of the murder of Lily Griffiths. Executed at Cardiff, 5 September 1945. The identity of the hangman is not recorded.

Thomas Richardson, age 27, convicted of the murder of David Dewar. Executed at Leeds, 7 September 1945. Hangman: Thomas Pierrepoint.

Joachim Goltz, Josep Martins, Heintz Brueling, Erich Keonig and Kurt Zuchlsdoff, ages not recorded, convicted of the murder of Sergeant Major Wolfgang Rosterg. Executed at Pentonville, 6 October 1945. Hangman: Albert Pierrepoint.

The five condemned men had been prisoners of war in the Comrie Camp in Perthshire, and on the morning of 23 December 1944 they had dragged fellow prisoner, Wolfgang Rosterg, from bed, beaten him severely, and then hanged him in a latrine. Their justification for this was, they claimed, that he was a traitor to Germany and deserved to die.

Ronald Bertam Mauri, age 32, convicted of the murder of girlfriend Vera Guest. Executed at Wandsworth, 31 October 1945. Hangman: Albert Pierrepoint.

Armin Kuehne and Emil Schmittendorf, ages 21 and 31, jointly convicted of the murder of Gerhardt Rettig. Executed at Pentonville, 16 November 1945. Hangman: Albert Pierrepoint.

The two condemned men were prisoners of war at a camp near Sheffield, and on the morning of 24 March 1945 they battered fellow prisoner Gerhardt Rettig to death because they believed he had informed on an escape attempt.

John Amery, age 33, convicted of treason. Executed at Wandsworth, 19 December 1945. Hangman: Albert Pierrepoint.

James McNicol, age 30, convicted of the murder of Donald Kirkaldie. Executed at Pentonville, 21 December 1945. Hangman: Albert Pierrepoint.

John Young, age 40, convicted of the murders of Frederick and Cissie Lucas. Executed at Pentonville, 21 December 1945. Hangman: Albert Pierrepoint.

Reginald Johnson, age 24, convicted of the murder of John Ritchie. Executed at Wandsworth, 29 December 1945. Hangman: Albert Pierrepoint.

1946

William Joyce, age 39, convicted of treason. Executed at Wandsworth, 3 January 1946. Hangman: Albert Pierrepoint.

William Joyce was born in Brooklyn, New York, but held a British passport because he claimed on his application to have been born in Galway, Ireland, thus making him a British citizen. In 1933, then living in Penarth, he joined the British Fascist movement, but in 1937 he left the organisation and formed his own movement, the National Socialist League, which would be outlawed shortly before the outbreak of war with Germany in 1939.

Sensing war was inevitable, Joyce went to Germany and offered his services to the Nazis. He was next heard of using the call sign Lord Haw Haw for his *Germany Calling* broadcasts which he kept up throughout the war. The broadcasts, propaganda for the Nazis, were intended to influence the British people into questioning the struggle their government had thrown them into. But in truth few people in Britain took Lord Haw Haw seriously and he became a figure of fun.

Theodore William Schurch, age 27, convicted of treason. Executed at Pentonville, 4 January 1946. Hangman: Albert Pierrepoint.

Schurch, born in London of Swiss parents, was a supporter of the Nazi ideology. He has been overshadowed in history by William Joyce, Lord Haw Haw, who was hanged the day before him. Schurch was the last man to be executed for treason in the UK.

William Batty, age 27, convicted of the murder of Samuel Gray. Executed at Leeds, 8 January 1946. Hangman: Thomas Pierrepoint.

Michael Niescior, age 29, convicted of the murder of Charles Elphick. Executed at Wandsworth, 31 January 1946. Hangman: Albert Pierrepoint.

John Lyon, age 21, convicted of the murder of John Brady. Executed at Glasgow, 8 February 1946. Hangman: Albert Pierrepoint.

Charles Prescott, age 23, convicted of the murder of Sarah Jean Young. Executed at Durham, 5 March 1946. Hangman: Thomas Pierrepoint.

Arthur Clegg, age 42, convicted of the murder of granddaughter Jill Clegg. Executed at Wandsworth, 19 March 1946. Hangman: Albert Pierrepoint.

Arthur Charles, age 34, convicted of the murder of John Duplessis. Executed at Durham, 26 March 1946. Hangman: Stephen Wade.

Marion Grondkowski and Henryk Malinowski, ages 32 and 24, jointly convicted of the murder of Reuben Martirosoff. Executed at Wandsworth, 2 April 1946. Hangman: Albert Pierrepoint.

Patrick Carraher, age 39, convicted of the murder of John Gordon. Executed at Glasgow, 6 April 1946. The identity of the hangman is not recorded.

Harold Berry, age 30, convicted of the murder of Bernard Phillips. Executed at Manchester, 9 April 1946. The identity of the hangman is not recorded.

Martin Patrick Coffey, age 24, convicted of the murder of Henry Dutton. Executed at Manchester, 24 April 1946. The identity of the hangman is not recorded.

Leonard Holmes, age, 32, convicted of the murder of wife Peggy Agnes. Executed at Lincoln, 28 May 1946. The identity of the hangman is not recorded.

Thomas Hendren, age 31, convicted of the murder of girlfriend Ella Valentine Staunton. Executed at Liverpool, 17 July 1946.

Walter Clayton, age 22, convicted of the murder of girlfriend Joyce Jacques. Executed at Liverpool, 7 August 1946. Hangman: Albert Pierrepoint.

John Caldwell, age 20, convicted of the murder of James Stratten. Executed at Glasgow, 10 August 1946. Hangman: Albert Pierrepoint.

Sydney John Smith, age 24, convicted of the murder of John Whatman. Executed at Wandsworth, 6 September 1946. Hangman: Albert Pierrepoint.

David Baillie Mason, age 39, convicted of the murder of wife Dorothy. Executed at Wandsworth, 6 September 1946. Hangman: Albert Pierrepoint.

Neville George Heath, age 28, convicted of the murder of girlfriend Margery Brownell and Doreen Marshall. Executed at Pentonville, 16 October 1946. Hangman: Albert Pierrepoint.

Arthur Robert Boyce, age 45, convicted of the murder of girlfriend Elizabeth McLindon. Executed at Pentonville, 1 November 1946. Hangman: Albert Pierrepoint.

Frank Freiyer, age 26, convicted of the murder of girlfriend Joyce Brierley. Executed at Wandsworth, 13 November 1946. Hangman: Albert Pierrepoint.

Arthur Rushton, age 31, convicted of the murder of girlfriend Catherine Cooper. Executed at Liverpool, 19 November 1946. The identity of the hangman is not recorded.

John Mathieson, age 23, convicted of the murder of Mona Vanderstay. Executed at Pentonville, 10 December 1946. Hangman: Albert Pierrepoint.

1947

Stanley Sheminant, age 28, convicted of the murder of Harry Berrisford. Executed at Liverpool, 3 January 1947. The identity of the hangman is not recorded.

Albert Sabin, age 21, convicted of the murder of Neil Macleod. Executed at Leeds, 3 January 1947. Hangman: Stephen Wade.

Walter Graham Rowland, age 39, convicted of the murder of Olive Balchin. Executed at Manchester, 27 February 1947. Hangman: Albert Pierrepoint.

Harold Hagger, age 45, convicted of the murder of Dagmar Petrzywalkski. Executed at Wandsworth, 18 March 1947. Hangman: Albert Pierrepoint.

Frederick William Reynolds, age 39, convicted of the murder of girlfriend Beatrice Greenberg. Executed at Pentonville, 26 March 1947. Hangman: Albert Pierrepoint.

David John Williams, age 26, convicted of the murder of wife Margaret. Executed at Wandsworth, 15 April 1947. Hangman: Albert Pierrepoint.

Eric Charles Briggs, age 40, convicted of the murder of wife Gertrude. Executed at Leeds, 20 June 1947. Hangman: Stephen Wade.

William Smedley, age 38, convicted of the murder of Edith Simmonite. Executed at Leeds, 14 August 1947. Hangman: Stephen Wade.

John Edward Gartside, age 24, convicted of the murders of Percy and Alice Baker. Executed at Leeds, 21 August 1947. Hangman: Stephen Wade.

Christopher Garaghty and Charles Jenkins, ages 23 and 21, jointly convicted of the murder of Alec de Antiquis. Executed at Pentonville, 19 September 1947. Hangman: Albert Pierrepoint.

Eugeniusz Jurkiewicz, age 34, convicted of the murder of Emily Bowers. Executed at Bristol, 30 December 1937. The identity of the hangman is not recorded.

1948

George Henry Whelpton, age 31, convicted of the murder of Alison, Joyce and Maurice Parkin. Executed at Leeds, 7 January 1948. Hangman: Stephen Wade.

When Doris Corocan went to investigate why her next door neighbour's door was left open she walked into a scene that would haunt her dreams for the rest of her life. Not only were all three members of the Parkin family dead, but they had been hideously mutilated. Maurice Parkin, aged 16, was lying dead on the scullery floor with his trousers pulled down and his genitals missing. Police would later discover that his penis had been pushed into his dead mother's mouth. The other body belonged to 23-year-old Joyce Parkin and she too had been mutilated with a cigarette pushed into her vagina. There was no sign of a forced entry, which led police to believe that the family had known their killer.

Police would later arrest bus driver George Whelpton who had been courting Alison Parkin and he admitted the killings. He told police he had argued with Alison and snapped, killing all three members of the family, but he claimed not to recall inflicting the terribly cruel mutilations on their bodies.

Evan Hayden Evans, age 22, convicted of the murder of Rachel Allen. Executed at Cardiff, 3 February 1948. The identity of the hangman is not recorded.

Full details of this case can be found *Dark Valleys* (2016).

Stanislaw Myszka, age 23, convicted of the murder of Catherine McIntyre. Executed at Perth, 6 February 1948. Hangman: Albert Pierrepoint.

Walter John Cross, age 21, convicted of the murder of Percy Bushby. Executed at Pentonville, 19 February 1948. Hangman: Albert Pierrepoint.

Stanley Joseph Clarke, age 34, convicted of the murder of girlfriend Florence Bentley. Executed at Norwich, 18 November 1948. The identity of the hangman is not recorded.

Peter Griffiths, age 22, convicted of the murder of June Devaney. Executed at Liverpool, 29 November 1948. Hangman: Albert Pierrepoint.

George Russel, age 45, convicted of the murder of Minnie Lee. Executed at Oxford, 2 December 1948. The identity of the hangman is not recorded.

Clifford Godfrey Willis, age 31, convicted of the murder of girlfriend Sillvinea Parry. Executed at Cardiff, 9 December 1948. Hangman: Stephen Wade.

Arthur George Osbourne, age 28, convicted of the murder of Ernest Westwood. Executed at Leeds, 30 December 1938. Hangman: Stephen Wade.

1949

Margaret Allen, convicted of the murder of Nancy Chadwick. Executed at Manchester, 12 January 1940. Hangman: Albert Pierrepoint.

George Semini, age 24, convicted of the murder of Joseph Gibbons. Executed at Liverpool, 27 January 1949. The identity of the hangman is not recorded.

Kenneth Strickson, age 21, convicted of the murder of Irene May Phillps. Executed at Lincoln, 22 March 1949. The identity of the hangman is not recorded.

James Farrell, age 19, convicted of the murder of Joan Mary Marney. Executed at Birmingham, 29 March 1949. Hangman: Albert Pierrepoint.

Harry Lewis, age 21, convicted of the murder of Harry Saul Michaelson. Executed at Pentonville, 21 April 1949. Hangman: Albert Pierrepoint.

Dennis Neville, age 22, convicted of the murder of Marian Poskitt. Executed at Leeds, 2 June 1949. Hangman: Stephen Wade.

Bernard Alfred Peter Cooper, age 40, convicted of the murder of wife Mary. Executed at Pentonville, 21 June 1949. Hangman: Albert Pierrepoint.

Sydney Archibald Frederick, age 32, convicted of the murder of girlfriend Doreen Messenger. Executed at Winchester, 28 July 1949. Hangman: Albert Pierrepoint.

Rex Harvey Jones, age 21, convicted of the murder of Beatrice Watts. Executed at Swansea, 4 August 1949. Hangman: Albert Pierrepoint.

Robert Thomas Mackintosh, age 21, convicted of the murder of Beryl Beechey. Executed at Swansea, 4 August 1949. Hangman: Albert Pierrepoint.

John George Haigh, age 40, convicted of the murders of William, Donald, and Amy McSwan. Also Archibald and Rosalie Henderson, and Olivia Durand-Deacon. Executed at Wandsworth, 10 August 1949. Hangman: Albert Pierrepoint.

John George Haigh, forever known as the Acid Bath Murderer, was an English serial killer who, although convicted and hanged for six murders, claimed to have actually killed nine. Haigh misunderstood the term *corpus delicti* and believed that if a body could not be found then a murder charge could not be brought against him. His victims were either shot or battered to death and their bodies were then dissolved in a bath of sulphuric acid. However, when police finally caught up with him they were able to provide enough scientific evidence to secure a conviction.

'Mrs Durand-Deacon doesn't exist. I've destroyed her with acid. How can you prove murder if there is no body?' Haigh told the shocked policemen who had arrested him in 1949 over the disappearance of wealthy widow Olivia Durand-Deacon. The police had been alerted that the woman had simply vanished after a meeting with Haigh and, given his past criminal record, including fraud and theft, he became a person of interest in their investigations. The police forced entry into Haigh's storeroom on Leopold Road and, finding several items that had belonged to the missing woman, as well as a Webley revolver, several carboys of acid, and rubber gloves, they decided to arrest Haigh on suspicion of murder.

The police were not expecting the fantastic story that followed and Haigh confessed to having killed not only Mrs Durand-Deacon, but also the Hendersons and the McSwans. He also added another three victims, but the police were unable to substantiate these and so Haigh was charged with only six counts of murder. Now, in a bid to escape the gallows, Haigh told police that he had drunk the blood of his victims, that he was a vampire, and had suffered occasional blackouts since being involved in a motoring accident as a child. This was an obvious attempt to plead insanity, and the police would not believe it. They argued that Haigh was a cruel and calculating man whose motive for the murders had been financial gain. *The Daily Mirror* picked up on this story while the trial was still in progress and in a story published on 4 March 1949 they described Haigh as a vampire who drank the blood of his victims. The newspaper was held in contempt of court, fined £10,000, and the editor, Silvester Bolam, received a three-month prison sentence.

William John Davies, age 30, convicted of the murder of girlfriend Lucy Wilson. Executed at Wandsworth, 16 August 1949. Hangman: Albert Pierrepoint.

William Claude Hodson Jones, age 31, convicted of the murder of Waltraut Lehman. Executed at Pentonville, 28 September 1949. Hangman: Albert Pierrepoint.

John Wilson, age 26, convicted of the murder of Lucy Nightingale. Executed at Durham, 13 December 1949. The identity of the hangman is not recorded.

Benjamin Roberts, age 23, convicted of the murder of Lilian Vickers. Executed at Durham, 13 December 1949. The identity of the hangman is not recorded.

Ernest Soper Couzins, age 49, convicted of the murder of Victor Desmond Elias. Executed at Wandsworth, 30 December 1949. Hangman: Albert Pierrepoint.

Chapter Eight

Judicial Executions 1950 – Abolition

By the beginning of the 1950s the movement to remove the death penalty from law was gaining momentum, and although there were twenty hangings in 1950 and twenty-five in 1952, there followed a gradual decline in the death penalty being passed. There was a reluctance by the courts to impose the death penalty if there were other lawful options. Indeed in 1956 the death penalty was not used at all, there were only two hangings in 1957, five the year later, and seven in 1959. There was a total of twenty hangings between 1960 and 1964, and in that year the death penalty came to an end.

In 1955 Ruth Ellis, a single mother who had been trapped in an abusive relationship, became the last woman to be executed in Britain when she was hanged for the murder of her abuser. This provoked a public outcry against the death penalty. Two years earlier there had been a similar outcry with the hanging of 19-year-old Derek Bentley, a man who obviously had very little to do with the murder for which he had been convicted. And in that same year John Christie was hanged, which raised doubts over the guilt of Timothy Evans, the educationally challenged Welshman who had been hanged in 1950 for a crime that now looked certain to have been committed by John Christie. Indeed both Bentley and Evans would posthumously receive royal pardons, Bentley in 1993 and Evans in 1966. These three cases did much to bring about the Murder Act of 1965 which ended capital punishment, initially for a period of five years and then permanently in 1969. Each of these cases will be looked at in greater detail later in this section.

1950

Daniel Raven, age 23, convicted of the murder of in-laws Leopold and Esther Goodman. Executed at Pentonville, 6 January 1950. Hangman: Albert Pierrepoint.

James Frank Rivett, age 21, convicted of the murder of girlfriend Christine Ruth Cuddon. Executed at Norwich, 8 March 1950. The identity of the hangman is not recorded.

Timothy John Evans, age 25, convicted of the murder of infant daughter Geraldine. Hanged at Pentonville, 9 March 1950. Hangman: Albert Pierrepoint.

The case of Timothy Evans is recognised as one of the miscarriages of justice that led to the abolition of the death penalty. Indeed Evans would receive a posthumous pardon in 1966, but the Brabin Inquiry did not, as many people think, conclude that Evans was an innocent man. Instead it determined that Evans *did* probably kill his wife but that it had been John Christie who had killed his daughter. But as Evans had been charged and convicted of the murder of his daughter and not his wife, then of that crime he was innocent.

In was a cold, drizzly day in November 1964 when Timothy John Evans walked into a police station in Merthyr Tydfil. Police noted that the man looked tired, nervous and his eyes seemed to be unfocused. This was understandable given that he was about to confess to murdering his wife, Beryl.

The story Evans told police was that his wife had recently fallen pregnant, and given that they already had one child, a daughter, and were struggling to get by on the wages he earned as a van driver, they knew that they could not afford another mouth to feed. Beryl had suggested an abortion, which Evans didn't agree with, but he did realise that his wife was adamant they would not have this baby. Evans claimed that he had been in a transport café where he met a man to whom he spoke about his situation – he claimed not to know the man's name. The man sold him a bottle of liquid which he claimed would terminate the pregnancy. Then, the story went, Beryl had found the bottle and when asked what it was, Evans told her that it would end her pregnancy.

The next day, 8 November, Evans had returned home to find his wife dead. The abortion had clearly gone wrong and he now found himself with a body on his hands. He told police that he had lifted a drain cover outside his home at 10 Rillington Place and put his wife's remains down the drain. The Welsh police arrested Evans and telephoned their colleagues in London so they could check out the fantastic story. They immediately went to Rillington Place and found that it took four strong men to lift the drain cover, something the frail Evans had claimed to have done alone. They found no body in the drain, but they did establish that Beryl Evans and her daughter were missing.

When the Welsh police informed Evans that no trace of his wife had been found, he made a second statement and told a different story. This time he claimed that a man who lived in the ground floor flat at Rillington Place, one Reginald John Halliday Christie, had offered to help arrange an abortion. Evans said that he had gone to work, leaving Beryl with Christie, but when he returned he found his wife lying dead on their bed. She had been bleeding from between her legs and Christie told him that the abortion had gone wrong. They must conceal the body, Christie told Evans, or they would both go to prison. Evans then went on to say that Christie told him he would put Beryl's body in the vacant flat on the first floor, and then after dark put her body down the drain outside the property. Christie also told the shocked Welshman that he knew a couple in East Acton who would look after the infant Geraldine and raise her as their own.

Evans was now taken back to London for more questioning, but by the time he arrived the police had discovered the bodies of his wife and daughter, wrapped in a green tablecloth in a wash-house in the back garden of Rillington Place. Both had been strangled with some kind of ligature. In Geraldine's case a tie had been used and was still around the child's neck

Evans then made a third statement in which he confessed to killing both his wife and child, but the police made the decision to charge him with the murder of his daughter only. Probably the police thought that if they had charged Evans with the murder of his wife, then there was a slim chance that he would be tried for manslaughter and so they made the decision to charge him with the murder of Geraldine. This decision would have far-reaching consequences when three years later Rillington Place gave up its true horrors.

At his trial Evans gave yet another story and blamed John Christie for the murders, but Christie denied all knowledge of the crimes, and when questioned in the witness box he came across as a very credible witness. So Evans was found guilty and executed by Albert Pierrepoint.

But the story though was far from over. For the rest of the story, see the entry for John Reginald Halliday Christie on p. 120.

George Kelly, age 27, convicted of the murders of Leonard Thomas and Bernard Catterall. Executed at Liverpool, 28 March 1950. Hangman: Albert Pierrepoint.

Kelly's conviction was quashed posthumously by the court of appeal in 2003.

Piotr Maksimowski, age 33, convicted of the murder of girlfriend Dilys Campbell. Executed at Birmingham, 29 March 1950. Hangman: Albert Pierrepoint.

Walter Sharpe, age 20, convicted of the murder of Abraham Levine. Executed at Leeds, 30 March 1950. Hangman: Steve Wade.

Albert Edward Jenkins, age 38, convicted of the murder of William Llewellyn. Executed at Swansea, 19 April 1950. The identity of the hangman is not recorded.

Roman Redel and Zbigniew Gower, both aged 23, jointly convicted of the murder of Robert Taylor. Executed at Winchester, 7 July 1950. Hangman: Albert Pierrepoint.

George Finlay Brown, age 23, convicted of the murder of girlfriend Mary Longhurst. Executed at Durham, 11 July 1950. Hangman: Albert Pierrepoint.

Ronald Douglas Atwell, age 24, convicted of the murder of Lily Irene Palmer. Executed at Bristol, 13 July 1950. Hangman: Albert Pierrepoint.

John Walker, age 48, convicted of the murder of Francis Wilson. Executed at Durham, 13 July 1950. Hangman: Steve Wade.

Albert Price, age 32, convicted of the murders of wife Doris and children Jennifer and Maureen. Executed at Wandsworth, 16 August 1950. Hangman: Albert Pierrepoint.

Paul Christopher Harris, age 28, convicted of the murder of Martin Dunleavy. Executed at Glasgow, 30 October 1950. Hangman: Albert Pierrepoint.

Patrick Turnage, age 31, convicted of the murder of Julia Beesley. Executed at Durham, 14 November 1950. Hangman: Steve Wade.

Norman Goldthorpe, age 40, convicted of the murder of Emma Howe. Executed at Norwich, 24 November 1950. Hangman: Harry Kirk.

James Henry Corbitt, age 37, convicted of the murder of girlfriend Eliza Wood. Executed at Manchester, 28 November 1950. Hangman: Albert Pierrepoint.

Edward Isaac Woodfield, age 49, convicted of the murder of Ethel Worth. Executed at Bristol, 14 December 1950. The identity of the hangman is not recorded.

James Ronald Robertson, age 33, convicted of the murder of girlfriend Catherine McCluskey. Executed at Glasgow, 16 December 1950. Hangman: Albert Pierrepoint.

Nicholas Persoulious Crosby, age 22, convicted of the murder of Ruth Massey. Executed at Manchester, 19 December 1950. Hangman: Albert Pierrepoint.

1951

Frank Griffin, age 40, convicted of the murder of Jane Edge. Executed at Shrewsbury, 4 January 1951. The identity of the hangman is not recorded.

Nenad Kovacevic, age 29, convicted of the murder of Radomir Djorovic. Executed at Manchester, 26 January 1951. Hangman: Albert Pierrepoint.

William Watkins, age 49, convicted of the murder of new-born son. Executed at Birmingham, 3 April 1951. Hangman: Albert Pierrepoint.

Joseph Brown and Edward Smith, both aged 33, jointly convicted of the murder of Frederick Gosling. Executed at Wandsworth, 25 April 1951. Hangman: Albert Pierrepoint.

James Virrels, age 56, convicted of the murder of girlfriend Alice Roberts. Executed at Wandsworth, 26 April 1951. Hangman: Albert Pierrepoint.

James Inglis, age 29, convicted of the murder of Alice Morgan. Executed at Manchester, 8 May 1951. The identity of the hangman is not recorded.

William Shaughnessy, age 48, convicted of the murders of wife Marie and daughter Joyce. Executed at Winchester, 9 May 1951. The identity of the hangman is not recorded.

John Dand, age 32, convicted of the murder of Walter Wynd. Executed at Manchester, 12 June 1951. The identity of the hangman is not recorded.

Jack Wright, age 31, convicted of the murder of Mona Mather. Executed at Manchester, 3 July 1951. The identity of the hangman is not recorded.

Alfred George Reynolds, age 25, convicted of the murder of girlfriend Ellen May Larkin. Executed at Norwich, 19 July 1951. The identity of the hangman is not recorded.

Denis Albert Moore, age 22, convicted of the murder of girlfriend Eileen Rose Cullen. Executed at Norwich, 19 July 1951. The identity of the hangman is not recorded.

Robert Dobie Smith, age 30, convicted of the murder of William Gibson. Executed at Edinburgh, 13 September 1951. Hangman: Albert Pierrepoint.

John O'Connor, age 29, convicted of the murder of Eugenie le Maire. Executed at Pentonville, 24 October 1951. Hangman: Albert Pierrepoint.

Herbert Leonard Mills, age 19, convicted of the murder of Mabel Tattershaw. Executed at Lincoln, 11 December 1951. Hangman: Albert Pierrepoint.

1952

Horace Carter, age 31, convicted of the murder of Shiela Attwood. Executed at Birmingham, 1 January 1952. Hangman: Albert Pierrepoint.

Alfred Bradley, age 24, convicted of the murder of George Camp. Executed at Manchester, 15 January 1952. Hangman: Albert Pierrepoint.

Alfred Moore, age 26, convicted of the murders of Duncan Fraser and Arthur Jagger. Executed at Leeds, 6 February 1951. Hangman: Steve Wade.

Herbert Ray Harris, age 23, convicted of the murder of wife Eileen Harris. Executed at Manchester, 26 February 1952. The identity of the hangman is not recorded.

Tahir Ali, age 39, convicted of the murder of girlfriend Evelyn McDonald. Executed at Durham, 21 March 1952. Hangman: Albert Pierrepoint.

James Smith, age 21, convicted of the murder of Martin Malone. Executed at Glasgow, 12 April 1952. Hangman: Albert Pierrepoint.

Edward Devlin and Alfred Burns, aged 22 and 21, jointly convicted of the murder of Alice Rimmer. Executed at Liverpool, 25 April 1952. Hangman: Albert Pierrepoint.

Ajit Singh, age 27, convicted of the murder of Joan Thomas. Executed at Cardiff, 7 May 1952. The identity of the hangman is not recorded.

Backary Manneh, age 25, convicted of the murder of Joseph Aaku. Executed at Pentonville, 27 May 1952. Hangman: Albert Pierrepoint.

Patrick Gallagher Deveney, age 42, convicted of the murder of wife Jeannie. Executed at Glasgow, 29 May 1952. Hangman: Albert Pierrepoint.

Harry Huxley, age 43, convicted of the murder of girlfriend Ada Royce. Executed at Glasgow, 29 May 1952. The identity of the hangman is not recorded.

Thomas Eames, age 31, convicted of the murder of girlfriend Muriel Bent. Executed at Bristol, 15 July 1952. The identity of the hangman is not recorded.

Frank Burgess, age 21, convicted of the murder of Johanna Hallahan. Executed at Wandsworth, 22 July 1952. Hangman: Albert Pierrepoint.

Oliver George Butler, age 24, convicted of the murder of girlfriend Rose Meadows. Executed at Oxford, 12 August 1952. The identity of the hangman is not recorded.

Mahmood Hussein Mattan, age 28, convicted of the murder of Lily Volpert. Executed at Cardiff, 3 September 1942. The identity of the hangman is not recorded.
    The court of appeal quashed Mattan's conviction in 1998 after hearing that crucial evidence had been withheld at his trial.

John Howard Godar, age 31, convicted of the murder of girlfriend Maureen Cox. Executed at Pentonville, 5 September 1952. Hangman: Albert Pierrepoint.

Dennis John Muldowney, age 41, convicted of the murder of Countess Krystyna Skarbek. Executed at Pentonville, 30 September 1952. Hangman: Albert Pierrepoint.

Raymond Cull, age 25, convicted of the murder of wife Jean. Executed at Pentonville, 30 September 1952. Hangman: Albert Pierrepoint.

Peter Johnson, age 24, convicted of the murder of Charles Mead. Executed at Pentonville, 9 October 1952. Hangman: Albert Pierrepoint.

Donald Neil Simon, age 32, convicted of the murders of wife Eunice, and Victor Brades. Executed at Shrewsbury, 23 October 1952. The identity of the hangman is not recorded.

Eric Norcliffe, age 30, convicted of the murder of wife Kathleen. Executed at Lincoln, 12 December 1952. The identity of the hangman is not recorded.

John Livesey, age 23, convicted of the murder of mother-in-law Stephanie Small. Executed at Wandsworth, 17 December 1952. Hangman: Albert Pierrepoint.

Leslie Green, age 29, convicted of the murder of Alice Wiltshaw. Executed at Birmingham, 23 December 1952. Hangman: Albert Pierrepoint.

Herbert Appleby, age 21, convicted of the murder of John Thomas. Executed at Durham, 24 December 1952. The identity of the hangman is not recorded.

1953

John Alcott, age 22, convicted of the murder of Geoffrey Dean. Executed at Wandsworth, 2 January 1953. Hangman: Albert Pierrepoint.

George Francis Shaw, age 25, convicted of the murder of Michael Connolly. Executed at Glasgow, 26 January 1953. The identity of the hangman is not recorded.

Derek William Bentley, age 19, convicted of the murder of Constable Sydney Miles. Executed at Wandsworth, 28 January 1953. The Hangman: Albert Pierrepoint.

The case of Derek William Bentley became a *cause célèbre* and was seized upon by the abolition movement. It led to a 45-year-long campaign to win a posthumous pardon, which was finally granted in 1993, albeit only a partial pardon with the original conviction being upheld but recognising that the execution had been wrong. It was not until 1998 that Bentley's murder conviction was quashed all together. This finally recognised that an innocent man had gone to the gallows. The man actually responsible was 16 at the time of the murder, so spent only ten years in prison.

Bentley's pardon was delayed for many years due to political manoeuvring and pointless red tape, and when it did finally arrive it was a bitter-sweet victory, for Bentley's sister Iris, who had dedicated her life to obtaining a pardon for her brother and was instrumental in forcing the police to reopen the case, passed away in 1997 without seeing the fruit of her life's battle with the Home Office.

Derek is buried in Croydon cemetery and on his gravestone is written 'Here lies Derek William Bentley A Victim of British Justice'.

Bentley was born one of twins, though his brother died within two hours of birth. Derek was not expected to live but he pulled through. At the age of 4 he fell from the back of a lorry, striking his head, causing him to suffer from epileptic seizures. When he was 7 he was buried and had to be dug out after the air raid shelter he had been occupying was hit by a bomb. And when he was 11 his family home was destroyed by one of Hitler's new flying bombs.

In 1948 he had his first brush with the law when he was arrested for shop breaking and theft. He was bound over for two years. That year he left school, but soon found himself in trouble for taking away tools that had been left on a bombsite. At the age of 14 he was sent to an approved school in Bristol, where his mental capabilities were assessed: he had an IQ of 60, a mental age of 10, and a reading age of 4½ – in the language of the time, he was borderline feeble minded.

In 1950 Bentley was released and returned home to his family where he mostly kept himself to himself. His father managed to find him a job as a furniture mover with the Albert Hutchins Company, but this did not last long when a back injury led to him having to give the job up. It was now 1952 and Bentley had already started running around with the teenage tearaway Christopher Craig. This was something that horrified Bentley's parents and he was told to stay away from the boy, but their worst fears were realised on the night of 2 November 1952.

Christopher Craig came from a good family but his elder brother Niven made his living from crime. Christopher idolised him and styled himself as a gangster in impersonation of his older brother. Then Niven was given a twelve-year prison sentence for a string of offences including armed robbery. Maybe Christopher had a hatred of the police because of this. 'I do not remember in 17 years as a judge a young man your age who has struck me as being so exceptionally dangerous. You are quite cool and cold blooded. I have no hesitation in saying, from my observation, that you would shoot down if you had the opportunity any police officer who was determined to arrest you,' the judge told Niven Craig at his trial, and these words would be remembered when just weeks later his younger brother Christopher did just that.

On the night of 2 November 1952 Bentley and Craig climbed over the gates of the Barlow and Parker warehouse in Tamworth Road, Croydon. Craig had decided on the spur of the moment that they should break in but across the street John and Edith Ware were putting their daughter to bed when she pointed out the two men climbing over the warehouse gate. They were clearly visible through the girl's bedroom window and her father called the police, reporting a burglary in progress.

The events that followed occurred on the roof of the warehouse and have been debated ever since. The basic facts though are that when the police arrived Bentley was immediately arrested by Detective Constable Fairfax. Craig then produced a gun and fired at the policeman, wounding him in the shoulder, and when a second police officer came out of the stair-head he too was shot, this time fatally. According to the police report, Fairfax arrived on the scene with a number of other officers. He climbed the gates and then the drainpipe that led to the roof. He identified himself as a police officer and arrested Derek Bentley. It was at this point, the police claimed, that Bentley shouted, 'Let him have it, Chris.' And Craig shot at Fairfax, hitting him in the shoulder. The detective continued to hold onto Bentley and a moment later a stair-head that led onto the roof opened and Constable Sydney Miles stepped out, only to be to shot in the head by Craig. At that point Fairfax and two other officers led Bentley downstairs while Craig continued to fire at the police. They were then joined by yet another officer, Constable Robert Jaggs and all of the police went back upstairs and rushed at Craig who had by now run out of ammunition. Craig jumped off the roof, landing on a greenhouse in the next-door garden and severely injured himself.

Another version of what happened on the roof came from Constable Claude Pain, also present that night. He said that he had not heard Bentley shout anything to Craig, but he was not called to give evidence at the trial. Also both Bentley and Craig denied that any such shout had been made.

The trial of Bentley and Craig opened on 9 December 1952 in front of Chief Justice Rayner Goddard, whose handling of the trial has been criticised ever since, with some going so far as to say Goddard was guilty of engineering the execution of an innocent man. Throughout the trial he interrupted, usually to stress a point from the prosecution, but his most telling display of bias occurred in his summing up to the jury. The judge picked up a metal knuckle-duster that had been in Derek Bentley's possession and described it as a fearsome weapon. He then slammed it down on his desk for affect. Bentley said the knuckle-duster had been given to him by Craig and that the younger man had slipped it into his pocket. The weapon had been found in Bentley's right-hand pocket when the police had searched him. Derek Bentley was left-handed.

There could be no doubt that Christopher Craig was guilty of murder, but Derek Bentley had already been under arrest for several minutes when the shooting occurred. Bentley also claimed not to have known that Craig had a gun and he was adamant that he had never shouted the words, 'Let him have it Chris.' There have been suggestions since that the police fabricated their statements, lying about Bentley shouting the command to his accomplice. This is curious given there had been a case in 1940 when two men named Ostler and Appleby were hanged for the murder of a policeman. The two men had also broken into a warehouse and it had been Ostler who had done the shooting, but Appleby was heard to shout, when the policeman arrived on the scene, 'Let him have it, he is all alone.' Did the police, determined that someone should hang for the murder of their colleague, remember this similar case and use it to gain the death sentence for Bentley?

After 75 minutes the jury brought in a guilty verdict on both men, recommending mercy for Derek Bentley. Craig, being too young to face the death penalty, was ordered to be detained at Her Majesties Pleasure and would eventually serve just over ten years, but Derek Bentley was sentenced to death.

There followed strenuous attempts to win a reprieve but it was all to no avail and on 28 January 1953 Derek Bentley was hanged by Albert Pierrepoint in what ranks as one of the most shameful miscarriages of justice in British history. Four of the policemen involved in the case received awards for gallantry: Fairfax received the George Cross, Harrison and McDonald received the George Medal and Jaggs was awarded the British Empire Medal. Constable Pain, who claimed not to have heard the words, 'Let him have it, Chris,' was not mentioned.

Miles Warren Giffard, age 27, convicted of the murder of parents Charles and Elizabeth Giffard. Executed at Bristol, 24 February 1953. The identity of the hangman is not recorded.

John Todd, age 20, convicted of the murder of George Walker. Executed at Liverpool, 19 May 1953. Hangman: Albert Pierrepoint.

John Reginald Halliday Christie, age 55, convicted of the murders of Ruth Fuerst, Muriel Eady, Beryl Evans, Ethel Christie, Kathleen Maloney, Rita Nelson and Hectorina MacLennan. Executed at Pentonville, 15 July 1953. Hangman: Albert Pierrepoint.

The controversy over the execution of Derek Bentley was still fresh in people's minds when the arrest of serial killer John Christie revealed yet another miscarriage of justice in which an innocent man had been hanged. In 1950, Welshman Timothy John Evans had been charged with the murder of both his wife and his daughter, and hanged for the murder of his daughter. The arrest of Christie and the subsequent investigation would reveal that Evans had in fact been innocent of the murder that cost him his life.

Christie had killed for the first time in 1943 when he strangled Ruth Fuerst while they were making love. He temporarily hid her body under the floorboards in the front room of his ground floor flat at 10 Rillington Place, but later he dug a hole in the back garden and buried her during the dead of night. His second victim was Muriel Eady, and this time he used household gas to knock her out – Christie had concocted an elaborate device in which he had attached a rubber hose to the gas mains and then sent it bubbling into a mixture of Friar's Balsam. He told her he had medical training and that his mixture was a cure for all ills, a tonic when one needed a little boost. His victims were all too ready to trust this seemingly mild-mannered and polite man. Once Muriel was unconscious, Christie then stripped her naked and raped her while at the same time strangling her. She too was buried in his back garden. In 1944, following a wave of bombing, Ruth Fuerst's skull came to the surface. Christie threw it into the rubble of a bombed house at 133 St Mark's Road and the skull would be assumed to have belonged to yet another unknown victim of the blitz.

For a number of years Christie did not kill, but in 1949 the opportunity to kill again presented itself. The year previously, Timothy Evans, his wife Beryl, and their daughter Geraldine, had moved into the top floor flat at 10 Rillington Place. The young couple had a tempestuous relationship and when Beryl fell pregnant for a second time she demanded an abortion; they could not, she claimed, afford another child. The arguments between the couple then intensified. It would all end in tragedy but what actually happened to Beryl and Geraldine Evans is still debated to the present day.

What is certain is that in November 1949, Beryl and Geraldine Evans were murdered and Timothy Evans paid the price for these crimes when he was hanged in 1950. At his eventual trial Christie would admit to the murder of Beryl Evans but denied having anything to do with the killing of the infant. Now it is believed that Christie was the killer of both mother and daughter. Christie had even given evidence at Evans's trial, informing the court of the arguments between the couple and when the death sentence was passed. Christie broke down in court, openly weeping.

After the case Christie settled down to an ordinary life, but in 1952 he killed his wife Ethel and then went on a killing spree. Ethel Christie was last seen alive on 12 December 1952 and it is not certain when she actually died. We do know that she was murdered and then hidden beneath the floorboards of the flat she had shared with Christie. Less than a month later Christie sold most of their furniture, keeping only a mattress, a table and two chairs. He then picked up Hectorina MacLennan and knocked her out with gas before raping and strangling her, intercourse taking place at the time of death. He then placed her body in an alcove in the kitchen. Within a month Christie had done the same thing with two other women: Kathleen Maloney and Rita Nelson. Their bodies joined Hectorina in the alcove.

Christie now decided that it was time to move on. On 13 March he sublet his room to a Mr and Mrs Reilly, taking a month's rent in advance. A week later he took the family dog to the vet and had it put to sleep. Before all this he had wallpapered over the kitchen alcove that contained the three dead women and simply walked out of Rillington Place.

When the Reilly's moved into the flat at Rillington Place they would later say that they noticed an unpleasant smell in the kitchen, but had no time to investigate since Christie's landlord Charles Brown showed up and informed them that Christie had no right to sublet the flat. The couple had no choice but to vacate the property and the landlord set about making arrangements for new tenants to move in.

A man named Beresford Brown was hired by the landlord to clean up Christie's flat and he too detected the now noxious smell in the kitchen. He noticed that the alcove in the kitchen had been papered over and when he tore off a strip of the paper he was horrified to find the corpse of a naked women hidden away in the darkness. The police were called and it was discovered that there were actually three bodies hidden in the alcove. It would later be established that all three women had been gassed and then strangled with a ligature, sexual intercourse taking place around the time of death. A further search of the room would reveal the body of Ethel Christie beneath the floorboards, but this time there were no signs of gassing or of intercourse having occurred.

The newspapers quickly picked up on the sensational story and 10 Rillington Place became infamous, with details of the macabre discoveries making headlines across the country and even being reported overseas. Christie was now staying in a Rowton House establishment in King's Cross – Rowten Houses were hostels named after Lord Rowton which had been built to provide overnight accommodation for homeless men. As soon as he saw the newspapers Christie decided to move on before the inevitable happened and the police came looking for him.

Rillington Place though had still not given up all its secrets and on 25 March 1953 police decided to search its gardens and two more bodies were found.

A week later, PC Tom Ledger was walking along the embankment near Putney Bridge when he spotted a dishevelled looking man standing by the side of the river. He questioned the man, who gave his name as John Waddington and said that he lived at Westbourne Grove. The policeman was not satisfied with the information and he asked the man to remove his hat. He now saw the man whose face had been plastered across all the newspapers – John Christie had been found.

At Putney police station, Christie was all too eager to make statements about his murders. He would later admit to murdering Beryl Evans, commenting, 'The more the merrier.' Doubtless he was hoping to appear insane and thereby escape the hangman's noose.

It would later be noted that Beryl and Geraldine Evans had been strangled with a ligature, which was Christie's method, though gas had not been used in either case. Donald Teare had done the original post-mortems but had not checked for carbon monoxide in the bodies, but experts at the time claimed that the signs of such poisoning would have been evident to Teare, and so it was said to be unlikely that carbon monoxide had been used in the murder of Beryl. This evidence though, presented by the prosecution at Christie's trial, is troubling since it suggests that Christie was only claiming responsibility for the murder of Beryl Evans in order to appear insane.

The jury took 85 minutes to dismiss the defence's claims of 'guilty but insane' and instead found Christie guilty of multiple murders, and the death sentence was passed.

Phillip Henry, age 25, convicted of the murder of Flora Jane Gilligan. Executed at Leeds, 30 July 1953. Hangman: Albert Pierrepoint.

Louisa May Merrifield, age 46, convicted of the murder of Sarah Rickets. Executed at Manchester, 18 September 1953. Hangman: Albert Pierrepoint.

John Owen Greenway, age 27, convicted of the murder of Beatrice Court. Executed at Bristol, 20 October 1953. Hangman: Albert Pierrepoint.

Joseph Christopher Reynolds, age 31, convicted of the murder of Janet Warner. Executed at Leicester, 17 November 1953. Hangman: Albert Pierrepoint.

Stanislaw Juras, age 43, convicted of the murder of Irene Wagner. Executed at Manchester, 17 December 1953. The identity of the hangman is not recorded.

John Francis Wilkinson, age 24, convicted of the murder of Miriam Gray. Executed at Wandsworth, 18 December 1953. Hangman: Stephen Wade.

Alfred Charles Whiteway, age 22, convicted of the murders of Barbara Songhurst and Christine Reed. Executed at Wandsworth, 22 December 1953. Hangman: Albert Pierrepoint.

George James Newland, age 21, convicted of the murder of Henry Tandy. Executed at Pentonville, 23 December 1953. Hangman: Harry Allen.

1954

Robert William Moore, age 26, convicted of the murder of Edward Wilson. Executed at Leeds, 5 January 1954. Hangman: Stephen Wade.

Czelslaw Kowalewski, age 32, convicted of the murder of girlfriend Doris Douglas. Executed at Manchester, 8 January 1954. The identity of the hangman is not recorded.

Desmond Donald Hooper, age 27, convicted of Betty Salina Smith. Executed at Shrewsbury, 26 January 1964. Hangman: Albert Pierrepoint.

William Lubina, age 42, convicted of the murder of Charlotte Ball. Executed at Leeds, 27 January 1954. Hangman: Stephen Wade.

James Reginald Doohan, age 24, convicted of the murder of Herbert Ketley. Executed at Wandsworth, 14 April 1954. Hangman: Albert Pierrepoint.

Albert John Hall, age 48, convicted of the murder of Mary Hackett. Executed at Leeds, 22 April 1954. Hangman: Stephen Wade.

John Lynch, age 45, convicted of the murders of Lesley Nisbet and Margaret Curran. Executed at Edinburgh, 23 April 1954. The identity of the hangman is not recorded.

Thomas Reginald Lewis Harries, age 25, convicted of the murder of uncle and aunt, John and Pheobe Harries. Executed at Swansea, 28 April 1954. Hangman: Albert Pierrepoint.

Kenneth Gilbert and Ian Grant, aged 22 and 24, jointly convicted of the murder of George Smart. Executed at Pentonville, 17 June 1954. Hangman: Albert Pierrepoint.

Milton Taylor, age 23, convicted of the murder of girlfriend Marie Bradshaw. Executed at Liverpool, 22 June 1954. The identity of the hangman is not recorded.

George Alexander Robertson, age 40, convicted of the murders of wife and son, Elizabeth and Alexander Robertson. Executed at Edingburgh, 23 June 1964. The identity of the hangman is not recorded.

William Sanchez Hepper, age 62, convicted of the murder of Margaret Rose Spevick. Executed at Wandsworth, 11 August 1954. Hangman: Albert Pierrepoint.

Harold Fowler, age 21, convicted of the murder of Kenneth Joseph Mulligan. Executed at Lincoln, 12 August 1954. The identity of the hangman is not recorded.

Rupert Wells, age 54, convicted of the murder of girlfriend Nellie Officer. Executed at Wandsworth, 1 September 1954. Hangman: Albert Pierrepoint.

Edward Lindsay Reid, age 24, convicted of the murder of Arthur White. Executed at Leeds, 1 September 1954. Hangman: Stephen Wade.

Styllou Pantopiou Christofi, age 53, convicted of the murder of daughter-in-law Hella Christofi. Executed at Holloway, 15 December 1954. Hangman: Albert Pierrepoint.

1955

William Arthur Sale, age 43, convicted of the murder of Dennis Shenton. Executed at Liverpool, 29 March 1955. The identity of the hangman is not recorded.

Sydney Joseph Clarke, age 33, convicted of the murder of Rose Fairhurst. Executed at Wandsworth, 14 April 1955. Hangman: Albert Pierrepoint.

Winston Shaw, age 39, convicted of the murder of girlfriend Jean Tate. Executed at Leeds, 4 May 1955. Hangman: Stephen Wade.

James Robinson, age 27, convicted of the murder of Mary Dodsley. Executed at Lincoln, 24 May 1955. The identity of the hangman is not recorded.

Richard Gowler, age 43, convicted of the murder of Mary Boothroyd. Executed at Liverpool, 21 Jun 1955. The identity of the hangman is not recorded.

Kenneth Roberts, age 24, convicted of the murder of Mary Roberts. Executed at Lincoln, 12 July 1955. Hangman: Stephen Wade.

Ruth Ellis, age 28, convicted of the murder of boyfriend David Moffat Blakely. Executed at Holloway, 13 July 1955. Hangman: Albert Pierrepoint.

'Six revolver shots shattered the Easter Sunday calm of Hampstead and a beautiful platinum blonde stood with her back to the wall. In her hand was a revolver.' Wrote the *Daily Mail* following the committal hearing for Ruth Ellis which was held at Hampstead magistrates court and took place the morning after the shooting of David Blakely. The Chandleresque prose the newspaper adopted perfectly summed up the way Ruth Ellis would be portrayed in the newspapers during the brief period between the murder of David Blakely and her meeting her own death on the gallows. Calm and expressionless, a femme fatale, a blonde bombshell, a siren – just a few of the sobriquets the newspapers used to describe Ruth Ellis in their reporting of her trial for the murder of her unfaithful lover. In the public imagination she was filed in the same category as Marylyn Monroe, Jayne Mansfield and Diana Dors, while her tragic relationship with David Blakely was being summed up as a true life version of the murder ballad *Frankie and Johnny*: 'She shot her man, cause he was doing her wrong.'

'She was a brave woman,' Albert Pierrepoint told an interviewer for Thames Television in a 1977 documentary. 'She never spoke to me. She just came to me and stood in position over the trap-door.'

She had been born in Rhyl, North Wales, and her actual name was Ruth Hornby, but her father, a jobbing musician, changed his name for professional reasons to Arthur Neilson and Ruth began to use this new surname. In 1941 Ruth, by then a beautiful young woman, began an affair with Canadian serviceman Clare Andria McCallum. This relationship resulted in Ruth giving birth to a son whom she christened Andria Clare. However McCallum was already married with a family back in Quebec, and after being posted to France in 1944 he went back to Canada, abandoning Ruth and his infant son.

In 1950 Ruth met and married the man who would give her the surname that would go down in history. George Ellis, a dentist, was recently divorced. He quickly became infatuated with Ruth and in November 1950 they were married. They had a daughter, Georgina, but the relationship was a disaster and the couple split in 1951. The infant child would be taken north by George for adoption, which left Ruth to return to the clubs where she had worked before meeting George Ellis.

In October 1953 Morrie Conley, who owned a number of clubs and had employed Ruth as a hostess for several years, offered her a manageress job at one of his clubs. Ruth was delighted and she took over the running of 'The Little Club' in Knightsbridge. It was here that she met David Blakely. The pair had briefly met before, at another of Conley's clubs, and they had exchanged words when, in a state of severe drunkenness, Blakely had insulted several of the hostesses. But this time he was charming, witty and flirty, and there was an instant attraction between the two. That night Ruth invited Blakely to the flat above the club and they became lovers. Ruth now found herself in a love triangle as she was already in a relationship with Desmond Cussen, an ex-bomber pilot who also frequented Conley's clubs. But the relationship meant more to Cussen than it did to Ruth and as soon as Blakely was on the scene Ruth had little time for Cussen.

Blakely liked fast cars, and with his friend and business partner Anthony Findlater he was designing and building a new racing car, which they named the Emperor. The building of the car was an obsession and drained much of Blakely's finances, which meant that he was always relying on Ruth for money. This didn't bother Ruth unduly, she was after all making a good living, but one weekend when she and David went to Buckinghamshire she became furious to discover that this man who she was to all intents and purposes supporting seemed to be ashamed of her. David went into a local pub but upon discovering that his mother was there he made Ruth wait in the car and brought a drink out to her.

In June 1954 Blakely went to Le Mans as a co-driver in the famous 24-hour race, but when he failed to return when he said he would Ruth once again took Desmond Cussen as her lover. However when Blakely did return he was soon hanging around with Ruth again, and once more they became lovers, leaving Cussen seething on the sidelines.

In October Ruth lost her job at the Little Club, which also meant that the flat which went with the job was no longer available to her. She was now homeless, so she and her 10-year-old son Andria moved into Cussen's flat in Goodwood Court. Blakely went into a furious rage at this, but for once Ruth ignored him. For a period it seemed that Ruth and Cussen were making a go of their relationship, which provided some security for Ruth's son. In February 1955 they rented a new place in the names of Mr and Mrs Ellis. The new home at 44 Egerton Gardens must have given the smitten Cussen the feeling that at last David Blakely was out of their lives.

But it was not to be. In April Blakely's car blew up in a race and for some reason he decided this was Ruth's fault. Around this time Ruth informed Blakely that she was once again pregnant, though there was doubt who was the father. Was it Blakely or Cussen? There was a furious row during which Blakely punched Ruth in the stomach, causing her to miscarry and bleed for several days. During her recuperation it was Cussen who cared for her, but David Blakely was never far from Ruth's thoughts.

On the evening of 8 April Ruth had been expecting Blakely to come around so they could talk. When he failed to show, Ruth telephoned Anthony and Carole Findlater, but was told that Blakely wasn't with them. But Ruth didn't believe the Findlaters and asked Cussen to driver her over to their address at Tanza Road. There was no talking Ruth out of it and Cussen dutifully drove the woman he was madly in love with to his rival – an altogether strange situation but such was the complicated life Ruth Ellis was leading.

When they arrived at Tanza Road, Ruth saw Blakely's station wagon outside the Findlaters' home. She was furious and grabbed Cussen's torch from the back of his car and walked over and smashed the rear window of Blakely's car. The police arrived and Ruth was told to go home, which she did but not for some time. She went to a telephone box and rang the Findlaters' home but the phone was put down on her.

The following morning Ruth again telephoned the Findlaters and once again the telephone was put down on her. Again she persuaded Cussen to drive her over to Tanza Road and while there she hid in an alleyway, watching as Blakely emerged from the Findlaters' house, an attractive woman on his arm.

The following day, Sunday 10 April, Ruth spent the day at home brooding over Blakely. That night, Blakely and a friend of his, Chris Gunnell, pulled up outside the Magdalla Tavern on South Park Hill. When the men stepped out of the car Ruth emerged from the shadows and called Blakely's name. In her hand she had a Smith and Wesson revolver.

Ruth Ellis fired six shots. She hit David Blakely four times, one bullet missed completely, while another ricocheted off a wall and struck a passer-by, Gladys Yule, in her thumb. The gun then clicked on an empty chamber. Ruth would later claim that she had been intending to use the last bullet for herself.

The story made the front pages of newspapers across the country and beyond. Its fascination would continue and Ruth's trial was analysed in fine detail in editorial after editorial. The letters pages too were full of her: some said that she was a cold-blooded killer who deserved the death penalty, but most said that she should be treated with compassion, that she was guilty of nothing else but manslaughter given the extreme provocation and cruelty she had suffered at the hands of David Blakely.

'When you fired the revolver at close range into the body of David Blakely, what did you intend to do?' Asked prosecutor Christmas Humphreys at the trial, and it is said that Ruth's answer all but sealed her fate.

'It's obvious,' she answered. 'When I shot him I intended to kill him.'

The jury were out for 14 minutes before returning their verdict of guilty of murder, and the judge then handed down the death sentence.

Ruth refused to appeal, and while awaiting execution she wrote a letter of apology to Blakely's mother.

She would make it clear that she felt she deserved to die for what she had done, and although the public were clamouring for a reprieve she seemed to have accepted her fate as being just and proper. Right up to the eleventh hour there were hopes of a reprieve, and thousands gathered outside Holloway prison to protest against the death penalty, but it was all to no avail and Ruth

Ellis became the last woman to be hanged in Britain. Albert Pierrepoint said she showed incredible bravery as the noose was placed around her neck and she was sent to eternity.

When Pierrepoint was driven from the prison, his car was mobbed by angry protestors. He was called a murderer, spat at, and someone threw human faeces over the windscreen of the car. Pierrepoint stepped down from his role as hangman a few weeks later.

Frederick William Cross, age 33, convicted of the murder of Donald Haywood. Executed at Birmingham, 26 July 1955. Hangman: Albert Pierrepoint.

Normal William Green, age 25, convicted of the murders of William Harmer and Norman Yates. Executed at Liverpool, 27 July 1955. Hangman: Albert Pierrepoint.

This would be Albert Pierrepoint's last execution, though he didn't resign from his role until January 1956, following a trip to Manchester for a hanging that was called off due to a reprieve at the last moment. It was then that Pierrepoint wrote to the Home Office requesting that his name be immediately removed from the list of official executioners. He gave his reason as not receiving his full fee as the result of the reprieve.

Corbett Roberts, age 46, convicted of the murder of wife Doris. Executed at Birmingham, 2 August 1955. Hangman: Stephen Wade.

Ernest Harding, age 42, convicted of the murder of Evelyn Higgins. Executed at Birmingham, 9 August 1955. Hangman: Stephen Wade.

Alec Wilkinson, age 22, convicted of the murder of mother-in-law Clara Farrell. Executed at Leeds, 12 August 1955. Hangman: Stephen Wade.

1956

There were no executions carried out in the United Kingdom in 1956.

1957

John Vickers, age 22, convicted of the murder of Jane Duckett. Executed at Durham, 23 July 1957. The identity of the hangman is not recorded.

Dennis Howard, age 24, convicted of the murder of Davis Keasey. Executed at Birmingham, 4 December 1957. Hangman: Harry Allen.

1958

Vivian Frederick Tweed, age 24, convicted of the murder of William Williams. Executed at Swansea, 6 May 1958. The identity of the hangman is not recorded.

Peter Thomas Manuel, age 32, convicted of the murders of Marion Hunter Watt, Vivienne Watt, Margaret Brown, Isabelle Cook, Peter James Stuart, Doris Smart and Michael Smart. Executed at Glasgow, 11 July 1958. Hangman: Harry Allen.

Mathew Kavanagh, age 32, convicted of the murder of Isaiah Dixon. Executed at Birmingham, 12 August 1958. The Hangman: Harry Allan.

Frank Stokes, age 33, convicted of the murder of Linda Ash. Executed at Durham, 3 September 1958. The identity of the hangman is not recorded.

Brain Chandler, age 20, convicted of the murder of Martha Dodd. Executed at Durham, 17 December 1968. The identity of the hangman is not recorded.

1959

Ernest Raymond Jones, age 39, convicted of the murder of Richard Turner. Executed at Leeds, 10 February 1959. Hangman: Harry Allen.

Joseph Chrimes, age 30, convicted of the murder of Norah Summerfield. Executed at Pentonville, 28 April 1959. Hangman: Harry Allen.

Ronald Marwood, age 25, convicted of the murder of Raymond Summers. Executed at Pentonville, 8 May 1959. Hangman: Harry Allen.

Michael George Tatum, age 24, convicted of the murder of Charles Barrett. Executed at Winchester, 14 May 1959. Hangman: Robert Leslie Stewart.

Bernard Walden, age 33, convicted of the murders of Joyce Moran and Neil Saxton. Executed at Leeds, 14 August 1959. Hangman: Harry Allen.

Francis Joseph Hutchett, age 31, convicted of the murder of John Perree. Executed at St Helier, Jersey. The Hangman: Harry Allen.

Guenther Fritz Podola, age 30, convicted of the murder of Raymond Purdy. Executed at Wandsworth, 5 November 1959. Hangman: Harry Allen.

1960

John Leslie Constantine, age 23, convicted of the murder of Lily Parry. Executed at Lincoln, 1 September 1960. The identity of the hangman is not recorded.

Norman James Harris and Francis Forsythe, ages 23 and 18, jointly convicted of the murder of Allen Edward Jee. Executed at Pentonville, 10 November 1960. Hangman: Robert Leslie Stewart.

Anthony Joseph Miller, age 19, convicted of the murder of John Cremin. Executed at Glasgow, 22 December 1960. Hangman: Harry Allan.

1961

Wasyl Gnypiuk, age 34, convicted of the murder of Louise Surgery. Executed at Lincoln, 27 January 1961. The identity of the hangman is not recorded.

George Riley, age 21, convicted of the murder of Adeline Smith. Executed at Shrewsbury, 9 February 1961. Hangman: Henry Allen.

Jack Day, age 31, convicted of the murder of Keith Godfrey Arthur. Executed at Bedford, 29 March 1961. Hangman: Harry Allan.

Victor John Terry, age 20, convicted of the murder of John Pull. Executed at Wandsworth, 25 May 1961. Hangman: Harry Allen.

Zsiga Pantokia, age 31, convicted of the murder of Eli Myers. Executed at Leeds, 29 June 1961. Hangman: Harry Allen.

Edwin Albert Bush, age 21, convicted of the murder of Elsie Batten. Executed at Pentonville, 6 July 1961. Hangman: Harry Allen.

Samuel McLaughlin, age 40, convicted of the murder of wife Maggie. Executed at Belfast, 25 July 1961. Hangman: Harry Allan.

Hendryk Niemasz, age 49, convicted of the murders of Hubert and Alice Buxton. Executed at Wandsworth, 8 September 1961. Hangman: Harry Allen.

Robert Andrew McGladdery, age 25, convicted of the murder of cousin Pearl Gamble. Executed at Belfast, 20 December 1961. Hangman: Harry Allen.

1962

James Hanratty, age 25, convicted of the murder of Michael J. Gregsten. Executed at Bedford, 4 April 1962. Hangman: Harry Allen.

The execution of James Hanratty, known as the A6 killer, was another case that sparked controversy and there is still a belief among some that an innocent man went to the gallows. Hanratty was convicted of shooting dead the scientist Michael J. Gregsten in a car and then raping Gregsten's mistress several times before shooting her.

The mistress, Valerie Storie, survived the shooting but was left permanently paralysed from the waist down. It was her testimony that was critical in securing a guilty verdict against Hanratty, but it was questioned by many who felt the supporting evidence was too weak to justify conviction. Hanratty went to the gallows protesting his innocence.

Hanratty's brother set up an organisation called the A6 Defence Committee to prove James Hanratty had been innocent. The campaign group contained several Labour politicians and was part-funded by the rock star and activist John Lennon. The journalist Ludovic Kennedy was also a vocal supporter of the campaign, and he wrote many articles asserting Hanratty's innocence.

In 1998 a police review concluded that Hanratty was wrongfully convicted and the case was sent to the court of appeal. Later, however, DNA evidence seemed to confirm Hanratty's guilt, and in 2002 the appeal court ruled the conviction should stand.

Hanratty's family continue to protest his innocence, saying that the DNA evidence is unsafe in that there has been contamination, given that the materials tested have sat in a police laboratory for over forty years. At the time of writing it seems unlikely that the Hanratty case will merit further reviews.

Oswald Augustus Grey, age 20, convicted of the murder of Thomas Bates. Executed at Birmingham, 20 November 1962. Hangman: Harry Allen.

James Smith, age 26, convicted of the murder of Sarah Isabella Cross. Executed at Manchester, 28 November 1962. Hangman: Harry Allen.

1963

Henry John Burnett, age 21, convicted of the murder of Thomas Guynan. Executed at Aberdeen, 15 August 1963. Hangman: Harry Allen.

Russel Pascoe and Dennis John Whitty, ages 24 and 22. Jointly convicted of the murder of William Rowe. Executed at Bristol, 17 December 1963. Hangman: Harry Allen.

1964

Peter Anthony Allen and Gwynne Owen Evans, aged 21 and 24, executed at Liverpool and Manchester, 13 August 1964. Hangmen: Robert Leslie Stuart and Harry Allen.

Allen and Evans were hanged simultaneously, one at Liverpool and the other at Manchester. Although the two men didn't know it, they would go down in history as the last men to be hanged in the United Kingdom.

Total United Kingdom Executions During the Twentieth Century

England: 764 men and 14 women.
Scotland: 33 men and 1 woman.
Wales: 34 men and 1 woman.
Northern Ireland: 16 men and 0 women.
Channel Islands: 2 men and 0 women.

The youngest girl to be legally hanged in the United Kingdom was Alice Glaston, who was executed on 13 April 1546. She was 11 years old and the nature of her offence, probably petty theft, has been lost to history.

The youngest boy was John Dean, who was 8 years old when he was legally hanged for arson in 1629.

The gallows at Wandsworth Prison were maintained in full working order until hanging was fully abolished in 1988.

Afterword

The UK is unique in the path it took towards the abolition of the death penalty. In other countries abolition had followed revolution or liberation, as for example in South America; or legal challenges, as in South Africa; or, as in Eastern Europe, as part of a continental movement towards abolition. In the UK abolition was brought about by Parliament and driven by the consciences of certain MPs who took a political and moral stance. The was widespread outrage and disgust expressed following the cases of Timothy Evans, Derek Bentley and Ruth Ellis, as well as the crucial roles of such organisations as the Howard League and the National Council of the Abolition of the Death Penalty should also not be ignored.

The Howard League for Penal Reform, named after noted prison reformer John Howard, was established in 1866. It is still active in penal reform today and during its long history has played a key role in shifting the emphasis of prison from punishment to reform, has had a significant impact on the development of criminal justice policy, founded the national probation service, and was at the forefront of the ending of capital punishment in the UK.

The National Council of the Abolition of the Death Penalty was set up in 1925 and for many years it tirelessly campaigned to end capital punishment. In 1948 it merged with the Howard League, ensuring that abolition was at the forefront of issues right up until the 1965 Abolition of the Death Penalty Act.

During the first half of the twentieth century those agitating for the abolition of capital punishment were on the whole viewed by the public as cranks. They were typified by the eccentric Mrs Violet Van der Elst, who used to arrive outside prisons in her Rolls Royce on the night before an execution and spend the entire night singing hymns through a loudspeaker. The authorities viewed her as a nuisance and most people considered her something of a lunatic. However, she did keep opposition to the death penalty in the public eye.

When abolition did come, it is worth noting that it was a Parliamentary decision which was not supported by the British population at large. In fact, it came in the face of widespread support for the death penalty. This support has to some extent continued to the present day, but it remains unlikely that the death penalty will ever be reintroduced into British law. When Margaret

Thatcher became Prime Minister in 1979 there were several attempts to bring back capital punishment, but these motions were always voted down by an ever-increasing majority. There have also been regular calls from the public to reintroduce capital punishment, particularly following terrorist attacks or notorious murders.

Between 1965 and 1994 there were thirteen attempts in Parliament to bring back the death penalty, the last being held on 21 February 1994 by way of a proposed amendment to the Criminal Justice and Public Order Bill. The proposal was rejected in the House of Commons by 403 votes to 159. A separate amendment for the death penalty for the murder of a policeman was rejected by 383 votes to 186.

During the 1980s and 1990s many miscarriages of justice were brought to light and these played a significant part in changing the minds of many who had previously supported the return of the death penalty. Michael Howard is one, who during the 1994 debate was Home Secretary. He had long supported the reintroduction of the death penalty but told Parliament that he had changed his mind because of the realisation that the system could make mistakes.

Bibliography

The following publications, newspapers and websites have been particularly useful in the writing of this book:

The Encyclopaedia of Executions by John J. Eddleston (John Blake, 2002)

Britain's Most Notorious Hangmen by Stephen Wade (Wharncliffe Books, 2009)

Execution: A History of Capital Punishment in Britain by Simon Webb (History Press, 2011)

In the Shadow of the Gallows by Samuel John Hoare (Gollancz, 1951)

Illustrated Police News Archives

Capital Punishment UK (www.capitalpunishmentuk.org)

Executions Carried Out at UK Prisons

including the name and date of the final execution

Aberdeen – 1 execution – Henry Burnett, 15 August 1963

Armagh – 1 execution – Joseph Fee, 22 December 1904

Bedford – 7 executions – James Hanratty, 4 April 1962

Belfast – 12 executions – Robert McGladdery, 10 December 1961

Birmingham – 35 executions – Oswald Grey, 2 November 1962

Bodmin – 2 executions – William Hampton, 20 July 1909

Bristol – 13 executions – Russel Pascoe, 17 December 1963

Cambridge – 2 executions – Frederick Seekings, 4 November 1913

Cardiff – 20 executions – Mahmood Mattan, 3 September 1952

Carnavon – 1 execution – William Murphy, 15 February 1910

Chelmford – 9 executions – Charles Frembd, 4 November 1914

Edinburgh

     Carlton – 3 executions – Phillip Murray, October 1923

     Saughton – 4 executions – George Robertson, 25 June 1954

Exeter – 11 executions – Gordon Horace Trenworth, 6 April 1943

Glasgow

     Barlinnie – 10 executions – Anthony Miller, 22 December 1960

     Duke Street – 12 executions – George Reynolds, 3 August 1928

Gloucester – 7 executions – Ralph Smith, 7 June 1939

Hereford – 1 execution – William Haywood, 15 December 1903

Hull – 10 executions – Ethel Major, 19 December 1934

Inverness – 1 execution – Joseph Hume, 5 March 1908

Ipswich – 3 executions – Frederick Southgate, 27 November 1924

Knutsford – 4 executions – John Williams 19 March 1920

Lancaster – 1 execution – Thomas Rawcliffe, 19 March 1910

Leeds – 68 executions – Zsigia Pankotia, 29 June 1961

Leicester – 8 executions – Joseph Reynolds, 17 November 1953

Lewes – 4 executions – Percy Clifford, 11 August 1914

Lincoln – 17 executions – Wasyl Gnypiuk, 27 January 1961

Liverpool – 54 executions – Peter Anthony Allen, 13 August 1964

London

     Holloway – 5 executions – Ruth Ellis, 13 July 1955

     Newgate – 9 executions – George Woolfe, 6 May 1902

     Pentonville – 120 executions – Edwin Bush, 6 July 1961

The Tower of London – 12 executions – Josef Jakobs, 15 August 1941
Wandsworth – 117 executions – Henryk Niemasz, 8 September 1961
Londonderry – 3 executions – William Rooney, 8 February 1923
Maidstone – 11 executions – Sidney Fox, 8 April 1930
Manchester – 71 executions – Gwynne Evans, 13 August 1964
Newcastle – 8 executions – Ernest Scott, 26 November 1919
Northampton – 3 executions – John Eayres, 10 November 1914
Norwich – 11 executions – Dennis Moore, 19 July 1951
Nottingham – 8 executions – George Hayward, 10 April 1952
Oxford – 8 executions – Oliver Butler, 12 August 1952
Perth – 3 executions – Stanislaw Miszka, 6 February 1948
Reading – 3 executions – Eric Sedgwick, 4 February 1913
Ruthin – 1 execution – William Hughes, 17 February 1903
Shepton Mallet – 22 executions – Anicet Martinez, 15 June 1945
Shrewsbury – 8 executions – George Riley, 9 February 1961
St. Albans – 2 executions – George Anderson, 23 December 1914
St. Hellier – 2 executions – Francis Hutchet, 9 October 1959
Stafford – 8 executions – Josiah Davies, 10 March 1914
Swansea – 9 executions – Vivian Teed, 6 May 1958
Usk – 4 executions – William Sullivan, 23 March 1922
Wakefield – 10 executions – John McCartney, 29 December 1915
Warwick – 4 executions – Henry Parker, 15 December 1908
Winchester – 16 executions – Dennis Whitty, 17 December 1963
Worcester – 4 executions – Djang Djin Sung, 3 December 3 1919

Total number of executions relating to crime

Murder:		Treason	
England		**England**	
Men: 729	Women: 14	Men: 4	Women: 0
Scotland		**Spying**	
Men: 33	Women: 1	**England**	
Wales		Men: 25	Women: 0
Men: 34	Women: 1	**Rape**	
Northern Ireland		**England**	
Men: 16	Women: 0	Men: 6	Women: 0
Channel Islands			
Men: 2	Women: 0		

Index